COME TOMORROW

A STORY ABOUT GURKHAS AND THEIR LAND

Mani Dixit

COME TOMORROW

A STORY ABOUT GURKHAS AND THEIR LAND

by

Mani Dixit

ADARSH BOOKS

Previously Published by Sajha Prakashan in 1980.

COME TOMORROW:
A STORY OF GURKHAS AND THEIR LAND
by Mani Dixit

Edition 2000

ISBN 81-87138-16-5

Except for the historical references, all events and characters in this book are fictional any resemblance to any person, either living or dead is purely coincidental.

Publisher :
ADARSH ENTERPRISES
E - 22-C, Jawahar Park, Laxmi Nagar,
Vikas Marg, New Delhi - 110 092
Phone : 246 9733, 246 4961
e-mail : adarshbooks@vsnl.com
nirmal@ndb.vsnl.net.in

Printed By :
JAI SHIVAM OFFSET PRESS
A-252, North Vinod Nagar, Gali No. 5
Delhi - 110092 Ph. : 244 3860

Dedicated to those valiant Gurkhas who have at different times over the years laid down their lives for that elusive goal— peace in the world.

BOOKS BY THE AUTHOR

Fiction

+ The Red Temple
* Come Tomorrow
@ Over the Mountains
# Annapurna Fantasy
@ Conflict in the Himalayas

For Children

+ The Adventures of Chandra and Damaru - Two Boys of Nepal

Poems

The Avenging Ghost

Non - Fiction

The Quest for Health (Health Services of Nepal)

Published by:
@ Ekta Books
+ Pilgrims Book House
# Educational Enterprise
* Adarsh Enterprise

AUTHOR'S NOTE

First of all, I must say a word or two about the title of this book. It is common practice in our part of the world to say, 'Come Tomorrow' in different senses. In this book's title, the words are not, I repeat are not, used in the sense of being a skit on the usual, widely prevalent practice but rather as a look towards the future - a look to 'The Dreams of Tomorrow' or to 'The things to be done on the Morrow'.

My intention was to put down on paper what may have been day to day occurrences in the lives of certain individuals. Seeing that it covered a period of nearly seventy five years, it was but natural that I had to draw on various sources to provide some factual background for the novel.

It must also be noted that though I made specific references to the Kalibahadurs the Mahendra Dal, there were other Gurkhas too from Nepal and in the Indian Brigade who were all actively involved in the Two World Wars, Enough has been written about the others. John Masters, of the 4th Gurkhas, writing in his 'Bugles and a Tiger' about the period in between the two World War says, "The 1st Gurkhas were earnest, the 2nd idle, the 3rd illiterate, the 5th narrow-minded the 6th down-trodden, the 7th unshaven the 8th exhibitionist, the 9th Brahminical (they enlisted high class Gurkhas), and the 10th alcoholic" The-post Indian independence saw the birth of the British Gurkhas. Bearing all this in mind, I had to a certain extent taken an author's liberty, the novel was after all just fiction.

evail.

Come tomorrow is thus a peep into a interesting period of Nepalese history through the characters and the events of the fiction. However since the book was first published, a number of changes have occurred.

The country referred to as Burma by the British, officially reverted to the name of Myanmar in 1989. The capital too had its name changed back to the original Yangon. Other places mentioned in Come tomorrow, which had their names, changed at that time were :

Old name	**New Name**
Maymyo	Pyin U Lwin
Moulmein	Mawlamyine
Pagan	bagan
Pegu	bago
Prome	Pyay (or Pyi)
Syriam	Thanlyin
Irrawaddy River	Ayeyarwady River

This new edition of the book has had the names changed accordingly.

Under its new garb its title too has been changed to **"Come Tomorrow :** A Story about Gurkhas and their Land"

July 2000. **MANI DIXIT**

1

Hari Bahadur Moktan had served in the horse cavalry of the Rana Prime Minister since 1901. In fact his association with Maharaja Chandra Shumsher went long before that for he had been in the latter's household for a good thirty years. His father had been an athparia out there and little Hari being his only child had spent his time in Kathmandu. As little Hari grew up, he had been an errand boy for Chandra Shumsher. The day that Chandra Shumsher became Commander-in-Chief of the Nepalese forces, Hari's father had gone before his master to pay his respects. The usual tradition had been followed and after dropping the one rupee coin with a tinkle to the ground, the old man had brought his right hand with the palm facing inwards in front of his nose, in a kurnesh, and said beseechingly, "Raja, I have served you loyally all these years. This is a proud moment in my life to see you as Chief Sahib. I hope to see the day when you will be the Maharaja. May your Chief Sahib in his kindness grant my son service in the army, possibly as a havaldar."

The new Commander in Chief nodded his head and Hari Bahadur felt that his father's wish had been granted. The following day Hari Bahadur and his father went to see the kitapi khardar to acquaint him of the fact that the new C–in–C had made his first appointment of havaldar. The kitapi khardar heard them through and then only gave his opinion saying that this was next to impossible. After all Hari Bahadur having had no training was no better than a raw recruit. Furthermore, there was no vacant havaldar post not only in any of the eighteen paltans of Kathmandu but also not in each of the three paltans of both Lalitpur and Bhaktapur. When Hari Bahadur's father went and told this to the new C–in–C, the kitapi khardar was immediately sent for and told to arrange it somehow. There was no further argument. The kitapi khardar, standing on edge because of fear of the C–in–C made a note on his slip of paper and Hari Bahadur's father knew that his young son was in the Nepalese army. Noting could change that now.

It was therefore no surprise that Hari Bahadur started training for the army. This in itself was not hard for both he and his father continued living over the stables in Chandra Shumsher's house. It was occasionally that Hari Bahadur had to go for periods of training at the Tundikhel and then go back to his quarters and his duties at Chandra Shumsher's household. He was quite content as it is, for he knew nothing better. He marched, he pointed his wooden rifle at imaginary objects and occasionally charged with a group of his comrades, the length of the Tundikhel, brandishing his naked khukri and shouting the words, 'Jai Durga Mata.'

But the years did not have to roll by for it was a matter of months and came the day when Chandra Shumsher became Prime Minister in 1901. Hari Bahadur's old man had been right, he did not live to see the day. As Fate would have it, the long hot summer and the epidemic of cholera had carried the old man away. Anyway the kitapi khardar was sent for again and the new Maharaja told him that Hari Bahadur was to be made a jamadar in the army. The kitapi khardar brought his two palms together and said, "Maharaj, I can do it, but some of the others might feel a little sore about being passed over for promotion."

"You let me worry about those. Don't tell me I can't even appoint someone to such a minor post. After all, I am the Maharaja."

The kitapi khardar did not say anything but brought his hands together once again and quietly backed out of the room and out of the Maharaja's presence. It was a proud day for Hari Bahadur, dressed up in his finery of a red tunic, a long sash across the chest and riding the leading horse of the six horse carriage of the new Prime Minister. There in the open horse carriage was the Prime Minister with his new shreepech or headgear. True, it was smaller than the crown worn by the King or Maharajadhiraj, but it did not matter. Hari Bahadur was sure of one thing his day had come just as sure as the day had come for Maharaja Chandra and his sons. Others must be happy too— his thoughts turned to the two Mahilas— the Guruju and the Pandit and to others. There, sitting at the plank seat at the back of the coach was Dharma Ratna, clutching a cloth bag in his left hand. His right hand dipped periodically into it and extracting a handful of coins of various denominations, he threw it periodically both right and left. Shouts of 'Maharaj, Maharaj' reached his ears and boys and girls nay, men and women rushed here and there to lay their hands on one or two of the coins that had showered on or by their side. Then the journey to the tree in the Tundikhel, the 'Khari ko Bot', which had seen a lot of the historical happenings of the Nepalese kingdom. Then the darshan of the King by the Prime Minister. It was a memorable day by all accounts and when it finally drew to a close, Hari Bahadur was sure that he would not see another like it for some time to come.

Maharaja Chandra was a shrewd man who wanted to be remembered by all. He introduced some new innovations into Nepal. The motor car in 1907 was just one of them, but with this started the age of accidents when the car fell off the bridge at Balkhu. Hari Bahadur had been supposed to go on a joy ride on that day but because of the pressure of work had been forced to cancel his pleasure outing. It was a lucky shave. Undaunted by such misfortune to others, Hari Bahadur learnt the intricacies of the new fangled machine from his instructor at Lazimpat. After some time on the roads, the same instructor issued to him a paper of proficiency and Hari Bahadur, from that day onwards, became Maharaja Chandra's chauffeur.

Then in the April of 1908 when Maharaja Chandra set out for England, Hari Bahadur was in the party. The journey via

Bhimphedi and Raxaul, then to Bombay before embarking on the ship the 'City of Vienna' for England. On the eighth of the following month, the party finally arrived at Victoria station— the start of a two month visit to the country. Hari Bahadur remembered some of the places he visited— the review of the fleet by the Maharaja and the white cliffs of Dover were imprinted in his mind. What remained vividly in his mind of that English summer was the visit to Scotland and especially to Edinburgh, the city of the Scots.

The visit to England was followed by a trip through the continent— to Paris, Milan and Naples. To the Nepalese, the phrase, 'See Naples and die' brought memories of home. A slip of the pen and it might have been Nepal ! Then the boarding of the 'City of Vienna' once again for the return journey. The two additions on the itinerary were Tuticorin and Rameshwaram to wash away their sins before they returned back to Nepal.

Following the return to Nepal the next event of importance was the visit and the subsequent shoot of King George V to the Terai. Hari Bahadur has been deputed under one of the Maharaja's sons to collect various animals for the menagerie that King George V was taking back to England. A veritable 'Noah's Ark,' if ever there was one—the animals such as rhinos, elephants, tigers. leopards, bears etc. climbed in one by one.

Though others found Maharaja Chandra a difficult man, Hari Bahadur could read him like a book. Chandra Shumsher practised his policy of divide and rule as a fine art. He had probably got the idea from the British but now he could teach them a thing or two. For example he never met even members of the same household at the same time—he would be closeted with each individual member for some time. On occasions it led to instances of father against son, or brother against brother. Then there was the occasional practice of spot checking by no less a person than the Maharaja himself. One fine day, without any pre warning he would visit the house of those against whom he had had complaints or those who he suspected of misutilising their power or position. He was never really satisfied with the British and paid them lip-service only. Though he was a well-wisher of China at heart, it neither prevented nor prompted him to put off the visit of George the Fifth to Chitawan for a tiger shoot.

Thus by the time the First World War started on March, 1914, Hari Bahadur had seen quite a bit of service under the Ranas. His master and mentor was the first to declare whole hearted support for the British in their war against Germany. This was evident by the fact that by this time there were twenty battalions in the then ten regiments of the Gurkha Brigade. It was decided that to relieve the Indian Army for fighting duties, some 16,500 men of the Nepalese Army would go under the command of General Padma Shumsher to the North West Frontier of India. The Kalibahadur battalion was present amongst this lot. In the normal course of events, Hari Bahadur could possibly have stayed behind, for his duties were mainly at the Maharaja's palace, but it was in fact the latter's wish to send him, for he wanted Hari Bahadur to keep a watch on the doings of General Padma Shumsher. They did not see much of action, but it was four years of boredom and getting exciting news and wanting to fight but not being able to take part. So near and yet so far.

It was just a time of army manouvres. Most of the marching was done in the mornings for the day-time temperature was in the region of 115°F. The fact that there were very few natural covers such as trees and bushes made matters worse. The days were long and the usual routine was to make preparations, during the long twilight hours for the following day. This day's exercise would entail storming a so called 'fort', which invariably was some hillock, and to take it over after it had 'fallen'. They would be tired after this exercise, their lips would be parched and dry and taking the tumbler of water to their lips they would make believe that it was rakshi that they were imbibing.

The end of the war was a joyous moment for all. The army men being strictly Hindus had had to be virtually enforced celibates and were looking forward to the day when they would able to join their wives at home. Then an occurence which nearly delayed them was some fighting with the Afghans, to forestall their attempt to invade India.

One week before they were due to come back, a mishap happened. Hari Bahadur was leading a group of his horse patrol when without warning a big boulder came hurtling down the hill. The horse was knocked down—both its legs being badly broken. Hari Bahadur's right leg was crushed into pulp. He remembered someone trying a tourniquet. Next thing he knew was that he was in hospital and he was in severe pain. When he found out that he had had to have his leg amputated and in fact this is what had been done, he was depressed for a few days. It would have been better he thought to have been killed outright in that accident. After all he had no family, and who would marry him now. He thought of his horse, which he found out had had to be shot on the spot for this seemed the quickest way out for its agony. Could not the same thing have happened to him, and he be simple listed as a war casualty, though technically it might not have been so.

When the Nepalese contingent finally reached Kathmandu in 1919, Hari Bahadur's amputated leg had healed though he suffered tremendously as a result of the 'phantom limb' His army mates thought him to be mad until a kindly doctor told him that this had happened because though the leg was no longer there, the nerves were intact and carried up sensation. This was the reason why he wanted to scratch a toe that was no longer there.

When Hari Bahadur got back to his old quarters he got the gossip from his mates. The feeling of these stable lads was that Chandra Shumsher had to give the English his backing though he was sympathetic to the Indian cause. He had sent four students to the Gandhi Ashram. On the other hand Chandra could not afford to antagonise the British for he wanted them to acknowledge Nepal's independence and His Majesty as King and Head of an independent kingdom. It was also voiced that Chandra probably realised that once the British left India, then the days of the Ranas were numbered. Though Maharaja Chandra was an introvert who kept his own council, it was claimed that his most inner wish was to give power back to the King.

Even Hari Bahadur was aware of a certain change. He felt uneasiness and tension all around and had the idea that even those reaping the benefits of the system were not happy with it. The slow but sure wind of change in India, the publication of magazines and papers by the Nepalese outside Nepal made Maharaja Chandra rather wary. He tried to get the British to stop the tirade but failed. The Nepalese, out of reach of Chandra's hand, did not care to respond. To partly pacify Chandra, the British acknowledged Nepal's independence on January 19th, 1919. Following this, when the Crown Prince was born, the British had no objection to Chandra giving him a thirty–one gun salute.

When Hari Bahadur finally reached Chandra Shumsher s Durbar and the Maharaja heard his story, the latter pitied him although he did have a good laugh over the phantom limb episode. Nevertheless, the latter gave Hari Bahadur Rs 1,500, a grand sum in those days. Feeling as if Dame Fortune had smiled at him, Hari Bahadur decided that as he had been also pensioned off from the army, he would go to Dhading and buy some land there to start a sheep farm. Begging leave from the Maharaja, he went off in a palanquin type of conveyance to Dhading, and bought a piece of land nay, a whole hill–side, for the then reasonable sum of Rs. 400. It was a whole hillock bounded on one side by Rani's Land plus a waterfall like stream, on another by Bhakta Bir Kunwar's land, and on thc third by a deep ravine. Ths fourth side was Timilsina's boundary and along this was the obliquc road that led to other people's land. Further afield of all this could be seen the red earth of Pashupatitar and the Kholpu river way down below. It was called Sapkota's Hill, with a Sallaghari of pine trees, but the name would change in course of time to Moktan's Hill. He was sure of that. He had bought the land in 1921. Give it another ten years he thought.

As he left Kathmandu, Hari Bahadur, though an admirer of Chandra Shumsher was at a loss to understand him. On the one hand he was giving the British backing but on the other he was not truly happy with them. Maharaja Chandra wished to reply or give his point of view to the Nepalese who had left Nepal to set up residence in India and raise voices of dissent. He got a press and gave his backing to a Nepali magazine at Benaras, the present day Varanasi. This became, therefore, a sort of mouthpiece of Chandra towards the Nepalese residing out of the country. Coupled to this was the usual practice of not only not allowing Europeans, but also Indians, to visit Nepal without a special permit called "Right of Way" or Rahdani. The idea of this of course was to prevent any of the new and bright ideas flowing into the country to bring about the winds of change into it.

2

Once Hari Bahadur Moktan bought the land and tried to start a sheep farm there, he had no dearth of helpers. The reason was partly because there was a number of people who wanted to give advice, which was unasked for. Their intention was more to get to talking terms with Hari Bahadur; for, he was after all, a bachelor and with substantial funds at that. What difference if he had to move about on crutches? It was the more reason that he would need an active and able wife, who in course of time would most likely wear the pants in the house. And then of course, he would most certainly be able to father a child or two-there was no suggestion whatsoever, come to think of it, that there was anything wrong with his sex organs.

There was no possibility of Hari Bahadur doing a marriage by or elopement, for he was no whole limbed young chicken. He had had offers for young brides, but he did not want to marry a young girl for the simple reason that he felt that he would become a 'cradle snatcher' by such a marriage. His marriage was by arrangement. The girl had had a lover but he had joined the Indian Army Brigade of Gurkhas. After a period of training had been spent in India, and as the girl Beli later heard, her boy lover had been sent to western Europe- where that was, she did not know- but a comrade had said that the fighting had been severe. They had had to hide in trenches, and though they had had their khukuris, the fact that the Germans had repeating machine guns and trench mortars had made the valient Gurkhas the underdogs. It was thus at Loos, in France that Moti Goley of the 2nd Battalion, 8th Gurkhas was killed. Meeting the furious head-on onslaught of the Germans, it was no surprise that the mere youngster Moti was not among the forty-nine Gurkha survivors of the Battalion that day. So Beli had waited till the end of the war expecting Moti back. When she heard from the boy's father that Moti had been killed in action and that they had received official confirmation, she still hoped against hope that it was not true and that some mistake had perhaps been made. It was only in 1922, a year after Hari Bahadur had arrived at Chetrafal, Deurali, in Dhading and four years after the end of the war that she finally agreed to marry Hari Bahadur.

It was a simple ceremony even by the standards of the time. Beli remembered the day for it was on the actual day of Bada Dasain, the Dashami. Every one was busy his own celebrations so it was no wonder that Hari Bahadur could barely muster about ten people to come with him to go in procession to Beli's house. They had come to take her away and this they did not by force but as a bride, by mutual consent. The wedding ceremony according to the prevailing custom was at the little hut that Hari Bahadur had built on his Sapkota's hill.

It was a sunny morning and there seemed to be colour all around, for most of the guests seemed already to have finished their usual Dasain Tika and had the jamara tucked under their caps. It was a splash of colour all right:— and then to cap it all came the placing of the tika on Hari Bahadur's and his bride's head by the elder members of her family. Then finally the actual feast of rice, mutton and plenty of chang. Hari Bahadur seemed very happy, if one judged his happiness by the amount of alcohol that he imbibed. Beli had been rather worried, for in the state that he was, it was doubtful if he was in a position to consumate the marriage that same first night: but he had performed alright, albiet a little clumsily perhaps, due to the alcohol in his veins. From that day onwards however, he had almost forsaken all alcohol, and had been rather like a dog constantly tagging behind a bitch in heat. Since they were now married he did not have to worry about competition from any of the younger lads of the village.

It was no surprise, therefore, when Beli missed her next period— it was more a time of secret rejoicing on the part of Hari Bahadur, Beli and both her parents. It was crude to bruit such an occurence at so early a stage. Give it another month before the news is spread around, was what they all thought.

During the middle of summer of the following year, 1923, a son was born to Hari Bahadur and Beli. The grandfather was overjoyed, but being a rather unimaginative fellow, decided that the child should be called Aite, because he was born on Aitabar, a Sunday. So it was, and the new born faced the world under the name of Aite Bahadur Moktan.

The Hari Bahadurs were not doing too badly with the farm. By the following year they had bred quite a number of sheep, and were doing good business making rugs and the traditional Tamang jacket,– a jacket which all the villagers seemed to wear during the winter months. These sheep's wool jackets, either half-sleeved or sleeveless, but open fronted: plus the pashmina shawls made of the soft wool of the sheep, found their way to the Kathmandu market generally around Dasain time. The money earned from this undertaking was eagerly look forward to by the workers not only of Hari Bahadur's house, but also by the rest of the village. In addition, there were the other things they grew or made and sold at this time, e.g. the dokos (wicker baskets) loaded with guavas or tomatoes.

Hari Bahadur, Beli and Aite used to live in the room literally on the roof. The single buffulo and a few of the more fancied sheep used to be housed on the ground floor of that hut. Other remaining sheep were in a nearby hut. One evening round about twilight, when it was not quite dark, Hari Bahadur yelled from outside the hut for Beli to come down for one of the pregnant ewes was about to deliver. As little Aite was crying, Beli picked him up in her arms and hurried to meet her husband's call. It was then that she slipped on the very steep slanted stairs, the child fell out of her arms and on to the ground below. She too fell but fortunately not on the child Aite. Beli let out a yell of dismay and Hari Bahadur came shuffling into the room on his crutches to see Beli getting up in agony, but the child a few feet away, playing as though nothing had happened. It was then that Hari Bahadur decided to call his son Bir Bahadur or 'Double Brave'.

The business prospered, and Beli was also expecting again. When this second son was born, the question of a name came up again. A neighbour remarked, "You called your first child after Bir Shumsher. Why don't you call your second one after Chandra Shumsher? After all Maharaja Chandra has done so much for Nepal. Think of the abolition of the evil practise of slavery. Then the signing of the recent treaty with England a couple of years ago, in 1923, which, I am told formalises the fact of Nepal's independence. I believe too that we Nepalese can, not only be recruited for the Gurkha Brigade but also for the Assam Rifles, Kashmir Rifles and in the Burma Army. I tell you that with such a name, associated with Maharaja Chandra, this youngster is bound to get a good start in life."

Hari Bahadur took a couple of seconds to collect his thoughts before he replied, "I did nothing of the kind, my first son I called Bir for nothing happened to him when he had what could have been a serious fall from the stairs. I think that his name Bir Bahadur or Brave Brave is very appropriate for he is truly Double Brave. What you have suggested for my second son stands more to reason, because in addition to the arguments you have advanced, my father and myself have been helped by Maharaja Chandra. We spent practically all our lives in his service, and we have taken plenty of his salt. It would take another lifetime to repay all his kindnesses, big and small. I shall be proud to call my son Chandra Bahadur. In fact it is the least I can do in gratitute to the old man. I hear that he is now so thin and frail that he makes his body look big by wrapping a long patuka round his chest and waist, before putting on his uniform and walking firmly, with flared nostrils when he goes down to meet his public. There is I believe a heaven and hell difference between what he looks like, dressed in his room, and in public, and with or without the padding. I feel quite sorry for the old man too. I believe his main worry now is whether he will be remembered, by the Nepalese people, and will be succeeded by an equally able ruler."

Bhakta Bahadur, the local wit, now seemed to find his voice. "Not only that but Maharaja Chandra took the initiative to get national tunes made for both the King and the Maharaja. Don't you remember, they always used to play 'God save the King' formerely whenever our king graced an official function. Do you remember also that the British diplomatic mission in Kathmandu complained saying that as we were playing it quite often, from so near approximity to Lain, they had to stand to attention at very odd times, as when they were in the middle of dinner, or doing what not."

+ + + +

During the next couple of years, the two boys Bir Bahadur and Chandra Bahadur, as they grew up, were the focus of their parents' love. Whether it was because Beli had been breast feeding her children, it so happened that there was a form of natural spacing between Chandra and Bir. Now, also after a few years, she was pregnant again and this time the little girl seemed to have a name ready the moment that she appeared. It was but natural that the daughter of Beli. a variety of Jasmine (creeper) should be called Chameli or Jasmine.

Then one sunny Monday afternoon on January 30, 1934, the boys, now about 7 and 6 were playing in front of the local bur and peepal trees. The first inkling they had that anything was wrong was when the ground started shaking. Frightened, they looked across and saw on a hill top, houses collapsing like houses of cards. Their one intention was to hurry back to their home. Amidst all the confusion, they saw an old lady come out of a house carrying a bucket of water. While others rushed here and there, she started membling 'Jai, Jai, Ganga', and proceeded to pour the water over her body. The boys though intrigued, proceeded to their own homes. Great was their surprise to see that it was still standing— a survivor of the Great Earthquake !

A few days later the boys heard from their father when he returned after a day's trip to Kathmandu that the current rumour there was that all the destruction and devastation had been brought about by the British who had recently flown over Sagarmatha (Mt. Everest), the home of the Gods, in an aeroplane.

It was customary for the three children to play together at home. Generally however, whilst grazing the buffalo or the sheep, it would be the two boys who were together. They would fool around, make plans for the future or even just build castles in the air.

Bir Bahadur, "Come tomorrow, I am going to join the army and then go to fight in foreign lands."

Chandra Bahadur "Come tomorrow, and I am also going".

"You can't do that. Who is going to look after Ba and Ma ?"

"Chameli can do that."

Bir— "No, she can't. She is a girl and so small at that. If I go, Chandra, you have to stay here. Don't worry, come tomorrow, I will go as a lahure, earn money and send plenty back home to help you and father. Then I will come back too and we will not only have a big farm but we will be really rich."

Chandra, "O.K., O.K. Bir. Come tomorrow, we will get things really moving."

\+ + + +

Although the war had started on 3rd September, 1939, it was in fact some three months later that the villagers first heard about it. For one thing, most of the Nepalese serving in the Indian Army Brigade of Gurkhas had not been coming home for leave. Then began the whisperings amongst the village panchayat members or elders about the true state of affairs. Young Bir, a bare sixteen had heard these things from his father Hari and he in turn passed on the news to his younger brother Chandra, who was then just twelve.

One day 'the boys were playing on the hill-side which was their own plot of land, when they heard the regular Jhyaali (village crier) shout out from the hill tops that because of the war, a lot of the young men over sixteen were required to join the army. The village crier then went on to say that this was a massive recruitment for both the Nepalese army and the Gurkha Brigade. The Gurkha Brigade of the Indian Army, they heard was no mean force and consisted of forty-five battalions. Furthermore, Juddha Shumsher, the present Prime Minister had given permission for the Nepalese to go to India and even abroad to fight against the Japanese and Germans. In going overseas, the Nepalese personnel would not lose their Jat (caste) and would be able to come back to their villages.

As soon as the crier had moved no, both the lads rushed to where their father was and asked him what all this meant. Hari Bahadur in turn told them about the caste system—how it had been handed down over the ages, classifying people into four main groups and keeping them in four watertight compartments. He said that this was something which was not only practised here but also in the army. The regiment's Hindu priest, the bahun, used to look after all this matter irrespective of whether the army was in the barracks or on the march. He was the man who had to deal with births, weaning ceremonies and even funerals. The presence of this minister of God was nothing unusual, for after all even the British army regiments had their chaplains.

"Well Ba, I think that I will go to join the army."

"Look, you have just turned seventeen. Why don't you wait a year or so. After all, the war might be over by then and then they will suddenly find a lot of troops on their hands. This may mean that you will have to come back very soon to your village life."

"What if I have just turned seventeen, father, I look much older than my actual age. Furthermore because we Tamangs don't have much in the way of moustaches or stubble on our chins, they are going to have a difficult problem trying to find out my actual age."

Hari Bahadur felt that his son had virtually made up his mind. It would be no use arguing, he felt; so he went on to say, "What you say is true son, but you must remember that you are fighting the Japanese who are also of Mongloid stock. I think that unless one hears them speaking it is very difficult to recognise a Japanese, a Gorkhali or even a Chinese in certain instances. My feeling is that the Chinese have high check bones, the Japanese less and the Gorkhalis much less. From what my father told me, some of our ancestors came from Tibet and started living on this side of the Himalayas. Because our ancestors traded in horses, we were named Tamang, 'Ta' meaning horse and 'mang' meaning trader in the Tibetan language."

"How are we related to the Gurungs then father?" Bir asked, little realising that his father had cleverly changed the topic of conversation.

"Well they are Nepalese and they not only look like us, but a lot of their dress, customs and language is related to ours. But this is one of the ironies of the situation that, in the various battalions and even regiments, there is some sort of segregation. The Tamangs are mainly admitted into numbers seven and ten of the Indian Army Brigade of Gurkhas. This had tended to keep a section of the Nepalese apart in certain groups. Then, again, the caste system is something worse, but no one dares say anything against it, for our priests might get offended; and then when one dies, they might refuse to perform the funeral rites, and one would be damned for ever in hell. Think what would happen if you could not do my arghan."

"Why was the village crier carrying out about jat, when we are in fact Buddhists, father ?"

"Oh, yes we are Buddhists. We should have our own 'ghyang', or a Buddhist temple out here at Chetrafal, but we do not have one for there are not many Tamang families here. But there have been Tamang families out here in the past, for there are quite a number of hikis out here. You know that hikis and manis are built as memorials to dead relatives. I hope that you and Chandra will do one for me and one for your mother when we are dead and gone. And don't forget the feast. After all, the priests tell us that all this will bring us some merit in the life here after. Not only us but also you two, who have spent the money on all this.'

'Oh, father why all this talk of death ? You and mother are not going to die yet,' said Chandra.

'No, I hope not. I am only doing so, because there are not many Tamangs of our community here. Those who are here might not know everything. Only one thing both of us wish is that you should cremate us rather than bury us as was the old custom. The lamas will be there to see to it, and the jhankris will also be present to assist him. You can however turn to Tauke Tamang should there be any question as to what should be done. After all, he is the oldest of our lot here.'

The talk of Tauke Tamang brought to Bir's mind the thought of Fatteh, the son of the village mulmi. He knew that Fatteh also wanted to join the army, but how they were going to do it was a problem.

"But father you have not given me a firm answer about my going to join the army," reminded Bir.

"Well, Bir if you want to go, I will agree to it but I feel that you should go after Dasain. Take this year's Tika. and enjoy this year's festivities; for, after all, you might never return," said Hari Bahadur.

\+ + + +

One day both Fatteh and Bir heard that more recruitment was going on. Once their mind was made up, Bir decided not to take even his brother Chandra or mother Beli into his confidence. They were sure that they would both get in somehow, fof with the various requests for recruitment, the initial sanction for fifty battalions had been fully raised. After this; more men would be required for garrison duties in India, for armed police units and for the new parachute battalions.

Once the boys got to Kathmandu it seemed that Bir had lost his first flush of enthusiasm. There was some divergence of opinion too, after all the shunting and shifting around that they had done. They met an official recruiter, and it was he who talked Fatteh into joining the Indian Army Brigade of Gurkhas. This recruiter was an army pensioner and he took Fatteh to the Gurkha Recruting Depot at Kunraghat, some three miles from the town of Gorakhpur.

Bir, not willing to go to India, and now on his own, thought that he would join the Nepalese Army. He did not have much difficulty in finding the Tundikhel, the army parade ground in the centre of Kathmandu. There were other hopefuls there too, and as they collected near the Mahankalsthan, they swapped names and pieces of information, about whence they came.

In all solemnity, the raw recruits entered the hospital in single file—a ragged lot in all sorts of clothes and trying to march in style but out of step. Through the big wrought iron gates, the massive three storey building over-awed them. To cap it all, a statue of a soldier was placed right on top of that building. Then the medical examination by the doctors at the Tri-Chandra Military Hospital. This was done out in the open, with the aid of an orderly to enter particulars and make the relevant notes. It was more cursory than detailed, for the main object seemed to be that if the man had eyes, hands and feet, he would be fit to take a pot shot at the enemy. It was therefore not surprising that Aite, or Bir Bahadur Tamang got easily enough into the Kalibahadur Battalion. A few months of basic training on the Tundikhel, and the recruits were now ready for come what may. They had their rifles and their bayonets, and of course the trusted khukri of the Gurkhas was hanging by their sides. Even if their rifles and the bullets failed them, their khukuris never would let them down and they would be able to show the enemy a thing or two; at least if any lived to tell the tale, for each soldier was determined that he would put the khukuri back into its sheath only after having drawn some blood. Durga mata would surely see to that.

The first leg of the journey for the troops was to Raxaul. The old route, marching to Thankot, then past the sentry at Chandra Gadhi on the hill and then down the slope to the resting point at Kulekhani. It was in fact the same routine the whole morning–marching for about fifty minutes and then resting for the succeeding ten. At Kulekhani however, they spent a day, recouping and putting things in order, for it was after all the first time that many had marched so far. The next day brought them to Bhimphedi and after another day's stop, the thirty odd miles by truck to Amlekhganj. What a place ! Most had expected that it would be a sort of paradise, a settlement where slaves who had been freed by Maharaja Chandra Shumsher in 1925 had set out to start a new life with bright prospects for the future. But the Eden was anything but that— a dull arid region, almost desolate and bare with its haggard looking inhabitants. The ones who were there still seemed to be probably those who had been fortunate enough to have survived the onslaught of the mosquito, and specially the malarial parasites. Then the sight of the narrow gauge train, the miniature train of the Nepal Government Railway (N.G.R.) was a sight of wonder, trepidation or amusement to the eight hundred odd men of the battalion besides other attached personnel,

The entraining itself and then the chug-chug of the little toy train, proudly carrying the Nepalese troops to fight on the side of the Allied Forces was indeed a memorable occasion.

3

It was late afternoon when they reached the Brigade headquarters at Raxaul. With possible exceptions among other Nepalese who might have gone overseas, the Englishman who received them was the first white man that many had ever seen. A couple of days went by, arranging things, teaching the troops about loading and unloading in trains. Then on to Lucknow of the Indian Mutiny fame. Here it was just a matter of getting down on the platform and cooking food and eating it during the two hours stop. From there the troops– the famous Kalibahadurs– were railroaded on to Habelion, a place near Peshawar. It was the end of the train journey, and all the men were then taken on foot–real foot slogging–to Kakul via Abbotabad, now in present day Pakistan. This was a terrible ordeal for most, and the going was hard, with the hot sun and the suffocating heat of the air rising from the tarred surface of the roads, at Abottabad, the place where the English depot was at that time. But it was better and cooler when the troops camped out at Kakul. and it was a further pleasant surprise to the Kalibahadur battalion that the Purano Gorakha (P.G.), Bhairav Nath and the Second Rifles, with whom they comprised the Brigade, were also there.

A few selected officers from each of the battalions went to the Army School of Mountain Warfare at Abbotabad and they in turn came and taught what they had learnt to their men who were drilling and training at Kakul. After a period of about eight to nine months, the Kalibahadurs went to Peshawar, to join the Peshawar (Pesh) Brigade under the command of the British. A further nine months of training as a brigade in mountain warfare followed, before they were considered fit for their duties. The days were in fact quite dull, seeing that it was manouevres and further manouevres.

Then the news came, not as a bombshell but gradually percolating through that the allies had had a severe setback at Dunkirk. To many it was just unthinkable that the British should have suffered these losses. Had they not been told that the British would never be vanquished? After all they had vast resources backing them—the total might of an Empire on which the sun never set.

It thus came about that the Kalibahadurs only had to move from place to place to help in the war cause. They boarded the train at Peshawar and travelled through the hot Indian plains, dry and waterless, towards Kohima. As the men including Bir Bahadur and his new friend Jit Bahadur looked out of the railway carriage window, they saw no sign of the war that they had heard had been going on. When the train did get to Kohima, they were a bit surprised, for the initial plans had been to by-pass General Slim, Commander of the 14th Army at Kohima and the men of the Kalibahadurs had been expecting to reach Imphal. Reaching Kohima, they had to wait for a few days—three or four—whilst all the civilian trucks or in fact anything on four wheels- 'a chariot'- was commandeered to transport the troops. The hundred odd trucks, with the men and equipment was then under two Britishers- a Senior and a Junior Supervising Officer (S.S.O. & J.S.O.) who went by the names of a Scott and a McLaughlin. The Nepalese officers were under them and functioned more as a source of link with the soldiers. The journey from Kohima to Imphal was easy going as the road cut right through the jungle on a plain terrain. Not only that, but it was also even, and pitched. The big surprise still was that there was no sign of the war. After the first day's travelling, they stopped for the night, and some even went shooting animals. One of the officers had some terrier dogs, which he was keen to try them out as sporting dogs. These went into the jungle and were never seen again. Were they eaten by hungry wild animals such as panthers, or by the Nagas themselves, through whose territory they were passing ? These were the first casualties of the war.

After this they started moving by night convoys, with the head-lights of all their vehicles dimmed. The rolling hills in the distance, all covered with dense forests, made the troops feel as if they were at home. The morning mist rising from the vall-eys, and more particularly from the course of the streams, way, way down below, was exactly as it was in Nepal. They conti-nued their journey again, over hills and through jungles, passing a few villages on the way towards their destination, which was Palel.

The night marches was generally in groups of threes. It usually started at dusk and with periodic breaks every hour and a main break at about midnight. They usually covered anything from ten to fifteen miles per night. The cool night air was much more conducive to marching—a complete change to the conditions at Abbottabad where they had been trained. Whilst marching they were not so aware of the cold but they were nevertheless tired and when they finally rested at about 3.00 a.m. they were foot-weary and thankful for rest. Only on one occasion they did not march during the night, and the reason was the blinding rain that was literally flowing down from the skies.

On such marches through the jungles, they had come across only a few villages. This particular stretch of territory had been rather hard on the soldiers, not a few of whom had sore feet, and perhaps even 'March Fractures'. Finally Palel was rea-ched. It, too, was almost in the midst of the jungle and far remo-ved from the battle front. The twittering of the birds, the roars of the wild animals during the evening hours and the rushing of the water in the streams by which they camped all seemed to belong to a different world. Many of the men even learnt, or were taught, to swim out there. The thought that the Japanese were not very near made the troops sometimes indulge in some singing and dancing to the accompaniment of the mahdal.

Sitting by the bonfire in the Officer's Mess, one of the Nepalese officers was toying with all these ideas in his mind when he heard a voice saying, "What are you thinking so deeply about?"

"I thought that there was a war and I came here to fight. We have no sign of the enemy. Furthermore, after about one and a half years of training in mountain warfare, I am at a loss to understand all this. We are all raring to have a go but this certainly seems far removed from what we had been expecting."

The S.S.O. had a smile on his face as he replied, 'You can forget about your mountain warfare yet. There is no enemy near us at present. You came out here to build roads."

"Build roads. That's not our job. It's a coolies' job. How will I explain all this to my men who having come all this way, want to let their khukuris have a taste of blood."

"You won't have to explain to your men. You just order them and that is all. After all, this is war; and we are all helping in the war effort. You know that the General's wives in England are probably folding gauge dressings, rolling bandages or sorting blankets. It is boring, but it is nevertheless necessary. After all John Milton said, 'They also serve who only stand and wait'. We are doing a darn sight more than that."

Little effort was required to coax the men, and to get the work done. Trees were cut down, picks and shovels set to work to remove the stumps and level the ground and it was no surprise that in no time at all the Tambhu Road was made from the Indian side at Palel to Burma. This road went straight on to the Chindwin and subsequently further to the Irrawaddy.

One evening when the road had been almost completed, and the officers were again in their mess, the Nepalese adjujant Dambar Shah turned to the S.S.O. and said, "Well Sir, my men have virtually finished the road. Is that all there is for us to do? As far as I know, we of the Kalibahadurs are not supposed to cross the frontier of India and go into Burma. What if we see a Jap on the other side ? Should we let him go?".

"Forget about the rules. Here you go, kill the enemy and come back. We will sort out the matter later. You know, General Slim at Kohima was telling us a few months back about the importance of hitting the enemy hardest at the point where he is least expecting it. Don't worry about crossing the frontier. After all this is war and if it does come to that, I can always like Nelson turn my blind eye at the frontier and swear that I never saw you or your men go."

Just as the S.S.O. said these words, they heard the low whirr of an aeroplane. A moment later they were literally showered with pamphlets. Bir managed to find one of these and went over it slowly. After a lot of matter about how the Japanese were fighting a just war in driving these foreign masters from the lands of Asia, the paper ended by saying, 'Go back Gurkhas. Don't shed your blood as paid slaves for these foreign masters. They will not be with you always. Tomorrow at 8.35 a.m. sharp we are going to make it rain bullets and bombs. Make sure you are not here'.

The next morning, the cooks got up extra early and by seven everyone had eaten and scattered into the jungle as per the plan. The Kalibahadurs did not have anti-aircraft guns but what rifles they had were pointed to the skies from the tree branches where they were hidden. Then at 8.35 sharp, a yellow plane came into view. It was carrying a loud speaker and as it went by, the Kalibahadurs could faintly hear the words, 'Farka Gorkhali, Farka".

Next there was a blue plane and this particular one flew over the edge of the jungle by the side of the road and sprayed some sort of liquid all over. Almost immediately after came the planes, perhaps some twenty odd ones, firing as they went and dropping incendiary bombs to set alight the areas of the jungle lying next to the road. As far as the Gurkhas, perched up on the tree-tops were concerned, they could not do much. There was no question of trying to bring down any plane. Round one had been won by the Japanese.

After this single episode, the days had therefore to be taken up with patrols and more or less sham fighting and manoeuvres. There was also practice in crossing the streams—not only by the men, but also for the mules loaded with the various equipment. Sometimes it was short forays in single file into the paddy fields. The object of all this, to turn the Kalibahadurs into a real fighting force, fit for jungle warfare, was soon achieved.

+ + + +

One coldish day in late October, news was received that one column of Gurkhas, after fourteen days of foot–slogging, had reached near the Arakan Range. A few had crossed the hill and reached Taung Bazar, and came back to tell their comrades. By this time, however, the news had reached Calcutta and perhaps Nepal and this particular group was called immediately back to the base at Calcutta. The matter was considered serious enough to have to be referred to Admiral Mountbatten, who was the Commander for the Allied Forces in South East Asia. The order was rescinded and the men involved started on their way back by steamer from Chandpal Ghat, Calcutta, to the base at Chittagong and then following the land–contour around the Bay of Bengal, to the R.A.F. Station at Cox's Bazar. From there they went on foot to Bawli Bazar; and when they reached it, they found to their utter dismay that the whole column of Gurkhas had been massacred by the Japanese. Their S.S.O. Harrington had been bayonetted and even the patients in the hospital had been killed. Their doctor, who was a captain had met his end in a burst of fire. There were bomb craters all around and even the usually hectic Taung Bazaar had a deserted look. The men who had been away were certainly lucky but the thought persisted in their minds that it was perhaps all the hullabaloo of the Gurkhas having crossed the Indian frontier that had most likely enabled the Japanese to break their telegraphic code, and then to attack the column. This group of Nepalese was then shunted from camp to camp until they were airlifted back to their battalion HQ at Kohima.

It was after this that the rest of the Contingent had any sort of taste of fighting. Three companies of Kalibahadurs in which there was Dambar Shah and also sepoys Bir Bahadur and Jit Bahadur were told one fine morning that they would be sent under a British brigadier for some action. They went to Shanshak and then to a place called Ukrul, both still on the Indian side of the border. It was through an area where there were trees on both sides of the road, and where there were no trees there were, however, plenty of scrub. They were moving on, and intended going further afield when it dawned on everyone concerned that they were surrounded by the Japanese. This was a difficult situation and seemed like one which would go on for some time, for the Japanese had the upper hand. It was tiring at night, keeping watch. The Gurkhas killed a few from the positions where they were but when this was told to the British Commanding Officer, he refused to believe it.

A little irritated, Captain Dambar Shah said, "If you won't believe us, wait till it gets dark; and I will get my men to bring you a dead Jap. to prove my words."

Towards dusk, Dambar Shah called Bir Bahadur who now, was no stripling youngster, but a full-blooded fighting man, and told him to take a couple of men past their own lines and bring back one dead Japanese whom they had killed that morning.

Bir Bahadur replied, 'Hunchha Saab' and went about his duties. He and a few of the men went stealthily into the dark forbidding forest. In a matter of a couple of hours, he came to report to Capt. Dambar, who in turn went to fetch his British C.O. When the two arrived, they found laid out for them to see not one, not two, but seven corpses. Examining one they saw tied to his belt some small 'ball' like objects. Opening one, they found within some boiled rice and pinch of salt. This was what the Japanese were fighting their jungle warfare on. For protein, they probably ate any small animal, or even snakes, they were able to lay their hands on.

Though the number of casualties was not much there was no ignoring the fact, nor closing one's eyes to it, that the Kalibahadurs were in a very difficult and unenviable position. Their water point was taken, they were low in munitions- ammunitions and rations. Fortunately they had wireless contact with Imphal. The planes, usually Dakotas, came and dropped ammunition, food and water on some selected and prearranged site. On one or two occasions they got stuff meant for the British troops, for besides the local British papers and paperbacks, there were also some tins of bully beef and the well-known 'K' packets. The sight of the parachute majestically floating downwards, bringing gifts as if from heaven, was always a great morale booster to all the men. The irony of it all was that only half of what was dropped fell within the selected site which was within the box formation of the Kalibahadurs, whilst the other half fell within the enemy lines. The Japanese were quite happy to let matters go on as before. There were content with the status quo, for with the Kalibahadurs surrounded in turn by them, it meant that they would always get a share of the dropping from the skies. Why look a gift horse in the mouth, although it was war, was probably what the Japanese felt.

After about a fortnight of this state of affairs, the Kalibahadurs felt that they had had enough and decided to move back towards Imphal. This was a retreat, and the place they actually came back to was a place with the high sounding name Yaingangpokpi, near Imphal itself. This objective was firmly instilled into the mind of each individual soldier before they actually broke up. They took most of the rifles and ammunition, but the heavy arms and equipment had to be left behind. Some took six days, some took eight, to reach their objective, while some fell a prey to Japanese Intelligence Forces (J.I.F.), and some got lost. It was a straggling lot that ultimately reached Yaingangpokpi. By a miracle, almost the whole group was there, except for the few who had probably been killed, and became the true casualties of war, so far. It was heaven ! These hungry men took double or treble of their daily intake of rice, with the resulting diarrhoea the next day.

It was not only the troops who started retreating. It was a mass exodus of the people of Gurkha or Nepali origin who made their way into India, with the intention of going back to Nepal. They made a representation to this effect to Maharaja Juddha Shumsher.

Events were going no better in Burma. True, the Gurkhas initially had the upper hard when they repulsed the Japanese at Pegu, the ancient capital of Burma. They had notable successes against the Japaaese at Prome, at Kyachse, at Monywa But all this made no difference, and it was the Japanese who seemed to be having the last laugh when the Gurkhas had to retreat back to the Lushia and the Naga Hills on the Indo-Burma border. The anticipated success of their operations Ha-Go and U-Go so bolstered up the Japanese ego that they developed designs of grandeur and planned their 'March to Delhi' a march which alas ! was never destined to take place.

Further successes of the Japanese at Rangoon, and increased skirmishes led to further panic amongst the local residents. People of Indian origins besides the Gurkhalis were also now involved. They piled into rickshaws and bullock carts or even trudged on foot on the long trail North towards Tambhu and the road to India.

Though this was a retreat into the expected safety of India, it seemed a journey without end. The wheel rutted track on the plains, the minor slopes which seemed gigantic in their tired state, the inadequate bridges which seemed almost too fragile to bear the weight of this retreating horde, and, of course the rain —the monsoon all played their part in making matters worse for the poor refugees, Before they turned in for the night, on the damp sodden earth, underneath any natural cover that they could find, they usually huddled around their cooking fires, exchanging experiences. They were full of tales of woe, of how their initial enthusiasm at the Japanese success which they hoped would free them from the yoke of the British, had been dampened by the haughty reaction of their new masters. There were horrifying stories of individual cruelty, and of brutalities and torture by the dreaded Japanese Military Police known as Kempeitai.

Bringing up the rear of these men were not, however the Japanese but the members of the British and Indian regiments including some Gurkhas. The monsoon— the life-saver of millions dependent on the land which had been an initial hindrance in the retreat, was now a life-saver once again, for it stopped both the land and air forces of the Japanese from coming in hot pursuit.

On the Gurkha side, of the men who had come from Nepal, the whole Kalibahadur battalion was regrouped and then re-equipped to fight and then sent off elsewhere. Though they were sent to various places such as Sitakuri, Nungtok, no actual fighting with the Japanese now took place. There were occasional patrol skirmishes. At Nungtok, a wireless message in cipher was once received, and then a Zitter attack i.e. firing without actual bullets took place!

Occasionally the Japanese tried to send in J.M.P. people. The Gurkha guard would say 'Halt'. The would- be intruder would reply 'Sathi' in Nepali and wait. The Gurkha guards, warned that the Japanese would try a ruse such as this, would not be taken in and would start shooting. A substantial number of such spies were killed off on a number of occasions.

\+ \+ \+ \+

Bir Bahadur lost his rifle and ammunition. He still had his khukuri, but he was then picked up by the Japanese. He was put in a truck and taken presumably to their jungle headquarters, God knows where. Even his trusted khukuri was taken away from him, as a souvenir and perhaps sent back to Japan to be a prototype for mass production in a post-war period. Would it henceforth be a Japanese souvenir, Bir wondered?

With an idea of 'Do or Die', Bir attacked his Japanese guard. The guard had tried to counter Bir's attempt at strangling him, with karate, but Bir had been quicker. He fled into the jungle and reached the safety of a Shan village. The villagers accepted him, and he stayed there in their midst, for the rest of the war.

It was more a sort of underground warfare that Bir was now involved in. True he was fighting the Japanese but this group of Shan people that he was with, had some sort of sympathy for the Chinese. Even during this time of war they were involved in smuggling textiles and other consumer goods right across Burma, under the very nose of the Japanese, and then across the border into the then Nationalist China.

Another sepoy, a friend of Bir known as Jit Bahadur, was rather a quiet sort of introvert lad. He too got lost but because of the fear that there might be Japanese about the place, decided, rather than risk everything, to stay just where he was, in the jungle. He had done his jungle survival course, and so he went very deep into the jungles of the Karen territory. He lived on the fish which he caught. He killed birds with catapults and caught small wild boars in pasos or snares. He was in fact literally a twentieth century Friday. One evening, he turned out his army knapsack inside out to dry. He found the few grains of wheat and making a clearing in the jungle, he planted these in the plot. It did not take long for the grain to grow in that environment, and he was able to grind the wheat grains in his helmet and make bread. Jit Bahadur's only lack in this life was that he had no one to talk to. These things just went on and on.

As the war progressed, General Slim took his troops to Mandalay. The Kalibahadurs, relieved because they had already had a stint of fighting were not kept on at the actual front.

The Mahendra Dal, together with the Kalibahadurs and Sher, had come to the Assam Front. The Mahendra Dal Battalion had been initially involved in taking over the oil fields and the pipes emanating from there. It was more a mopping up operation, flushing out the pockets of resistance of the Japanese, who had now turned tail and fled back towards the Burmese border. This was an easy task for the Mahendra Dal to accomplish. The real stuff started after the rout of the Kalibahadurs. The lot fell to the Mahendra Dal to continue or to finish what their predecessors in the field had started. Accordingly, the Mahendra Dal left their 6th. Advance Base at the tea-gardens at Dinza in Assam and went by jeeps, three tonner trucks and carted along on these, the mules, horses and tents. They went to Silchar, and then by train to Dinapur. From there along the Manipur road to Kohima and them Imphal. They were in their olive green uniforms and to prevent the Japanese from suspecting or guessing their true army ranks, all the brass insignia came off.

The real work started when they crossed the border and reached Homalin after an overnight journey. It was hilly country, much like Nepal and on arrival they were taken straight away to the rest camp. It was however a rest camp in name only. They were in a state of continuous tension, behind the stone walls and in the trenches. The men could not keep their weapons away from arm's length nor take off their boots for fear that the enemy might attack anytime. The unpleasant thought in their minds was that there was every possibility of dying with their boots on. From there the march led on to Tambhu and Indaw. They were lucky that to get to Indaw, the crossing of the Chindwin had been no problem. It was only when they got to Masein that they realised as to how big a river the Chindwin really was.

On occasions they would hear the Japanese signal, which was invariably a cock crowing. This the Gurkha troops always had a laugh about, for the usual consequence at home was to cut off the head of such a bird as it was considered unluckey to have it under one's roof. The Gurkhas went after such midnighs sounds, and usually managed to secure one or two heads as souvenirs to show for their trip. At other times, one would hear imitation of jackal sounds, Then one or two stray shots and then one could expect grenade fire. This was generally considered bad for one did not know where it came from. Fortunately for the Gurkhas, there were no serious injuries. Then the cannon fire—usually single bursts. The first shot was usually on the outer limit of the camp, the second shot was inside and then the rest of the shots, usually comprising some eighty to ninety shells in between. One or two fell into the trenches and the troops inside were killed. This fortunately was a rare occurance.

There was no holding The Mahendra Dal now. They went across the country, across the paddy fields and the jungles, across the mountains and the valleys to reach Myitkiyana and subsequently Bhamo. It was 'Ayo Gorkhali' all the way. Then came the Irrawaddy. An advance group crossed this on the five motor boats on hand, whilst the enemy on the top of the hill on the other side, shot at them. The men of the battalion covering them shot back with trench or three-inch mortars. When the Gurkhas reached the other bank, the Japanese completely demoralised, literally just fled. After this there was no problem of crossing the Irrawaddy. This was done and re-done in style, as practice on the rafts, amphibians like the 4-4 Dodge and motor boats. They then proceeded to Mandalay, the city on the river, founded some eighty years ago on the 2400th. anniversary of the death/nirvana of Lord Buddha. It was big but rather dusty. The onslaught began with the occupation of Mandalay Hill. This was easy enough for the Gurkhas. The more strenuous, exercise wise, was the mopping up of the Japanese troops who were in the underground chambers. It was quite an undertaking, as if one was smoking out the field rats out of a massive field, but it was well accomplished by the 19th Indian, the 'Dagger Division'. Then again cross country on plain ground most of the time with paddy fields on both sides, to finally reach Myothit.

By now a certain jitteriness had developed in the men of the Mahendra Dal battalion, for they were now meeting straggling Japanese soldiers. It was a case of now or never as they started from Allanmyo towards Prome. The real action came when it was decided to attack Mount Popa or Popa Hill, an extinct volcano, in what was known as the Kingdom of the Cobra. It was a red mountainside of sandstone and clay, with very little undergrowth or even grass. This hill was in fact the vantage point from which the Japanese surveyed the countryside of Burma. After three days of heavy fighting, in a three-pronged attack on Popa Hill, it was finally taken. It seemed that a few of the Japanese had fled during the night but the sight of the many dead was enough to give satisfaction to the storming Gurkhas. Those of the 15th and 28th Japanese Army captured as prisoners were sent, together with some men of the Indian National Army of Subhas Chandra Bose who had fallen into the hands of the Gurkhas, to the base camp. In fact, as the Japanese suffered reverses, the I.N.A. men, generally Bengalis came and surrendered their arms, ammunitions and themselves. In this actual onslaught of the Gurkhas it was as if Lord Pashupatinath was on their side for they suffered only minor casualties.

Such incidents were happening in many places in Burma as troops of the Allied 14th Army went forward and the Gurkhas within it distinguished themselves. A notable achievement was the thrust towards Pakokku and the fall of Meiktila, with its massive Japanese base and the numerous airfields around it. Then the tea gardens and finally the arrival at Prome, a small city, but beautiful, even at this time of war.

From there the road led on to Rangoon, a city somewhat reminiscent of Calcutta but with the golden spires of the pagodas. The house were not attached to each other and though the city seemed nicer, it was certainly not clean. There were tram lines but no trams, as these were not in use. The state of the city did not bother them much for The Mahendra Dal were not going to spend much time there. They were in fact on the outskirts of the city and after spending two days there, were due to go to Thailand on the third day.

Then came the Hirosima and Nagasaki horrors, and the unconditional surrender at Singapore of all the Japanese land, sea and air forces. The war was suddenly over. The Gurkhas of The Mahendra Dal never had to go to Thailand. They returned on a massive ship to Howrah and then by road to a joyous homecoming. The Gurkhas, all in all, in the total count of all the regiments, had paid a heavy price in this war, for it was estimated that out of a total of 100,000 men, some 10,000 had died and another 15,000 suffered from wounds and had to be invalided out of the army.

4

The War had been over for nearly a year when it was time to go for the Victory Parade at London. It was decided that the Nepali contingent from Kathmandu would consist of three general officers, three other officers and twenty other ranks.

The Nepalese troops had some initial arrangements and formalities to go through. First of all they were told by the Maharaja that they would not lose their 'Jat' as a result of having gone overseas. The Brahmin priests did special pujas and looked for an auspicious date on which to set forth for the foreign shores. The usual journey through Thankot, Bhimphedi, Simra and Raxaul. Whilst on the Nepalese miniature train, they saw the plane which had crash landed at the air strip at Simra, the air sleeve billowing out into the wind and so on. As they recalled in their minds the previous day's sight of the old Willys jeep's parts being carried on porters backs, over the Nepali hills, they too perhaps felt that Nepal was just a little bit behind the times.

Major Dambar Shah was among the lucky ones. The initial journey was to Bareilly and when the arrangements had been made, the group was called from Kathmandu to proceed by the land route to Mazaffarpur join up with the Indian contingent of the Indian army and then proceed on to Bombay.

At Bombay, the 39,000 tonner S.S. Mauretania was waiting for them and on this they sailed. It had initially been a civilian ship but was now doing this run for the army. The journey through the Suez Canal — where the S.S. Mauretania was a very very tight fit, was nerve racking to say the least. The twenty five days spent on the ship were not always pleasant for the sight of the ocean day in and day out did at times get rather boring to the landrubbers. As the ship docked into Southamptom, they all gave a sigh of relief and secretly thanked Lord Pashupatinath for having brought them this far without any mishap.

As the English train literally hurtled through the countryside the Nepalese brigade imagined that the British had had hard times during the course of this war. The devastation in the countryside was negligible in comparison to what they saw as they neared London. This was more apparent as the train came into Victoria Station, for it had been nothing but rubble, and more rubble, during the later stages of the journey. There would have to be a lot of rebuilding, was what everyone thought. However, though vast areas of the mighty expanse of London were utterly devastated, the fact that the war was at least over did create a feeling of comfort and happiness in everyone who had lived in this city. The Generals were then taken by car and the rest by military trucks to the Nepalese Legation at 12 A, Kensington Palace Gardens, a fairly massive structure, quietly tucked away in between numbers twelve and fourteen in order to avoid the bad luck of thirteen. So like the British, thought Dambar Shah, to have such a solution.

By the time that the actual day of the Victory Parade arrived, the representatives of all the Allied troops, excluding Russia, were there. It seemed to the Nepalese at Hyde Park that they were a source of attraction to the British. There certainly was a heroes welcome for the Gurkhas, the short statured valiant men from the tiny kingdom just south of the mighty Himalayas.

Then came the actual March Past down the Mall. The Kalibahadur contingent looked smart with their 'felty' caps on which had been placed an inverted 'V' on the right. Was this a symbol for the land of Everest? The Nepalese flag, the double trident showing the sun and moon, complete with eyes, nose and mouth was an attraction in itself. Then the 'eyes left' to the monarch King George VI who was standing and taking the salute. By his side on the dias was the Queen, whilst a little behind them both stood the heir apparent, the Princess Elizabeth. A little further back was the little Princess Margaret.

The troops marched on and into Whitehall. There at the other end of it were the famous Big Ben and the Houses of Parliament. The crowds of people, and the air of celebration, fully signified that London had now regained its gaiety. There were even plays such as the 'Worm's Eye View' in the Whitehall in full swing. Finally came the laying of the wreaths at the Cenotaph— a manifestation of thankfulness to the dead by a populace that was truly thankful. After all this, of course, later on in the day or after a few days, came the sightseeing of what remained of London. And it seemed at times that London was entirely undamaged ! On the other hand however other parts such as the Borough of Poplar was completely devastated and the only inhabitant that they saw as they passed by, was a stray cat. A few of the officers went to the Windmill — that theatre that never closed during all the years of the war. What was on at the theatre was of course a revue and the officers of the Gurkhas were shocked by what they saw on the stage. Or at least they said they were shocked.

A few days later the Nepalese Legation gave a party to all the Gurkhas who had come, not only from Nepal, but also as part of the Indian Brigade. The centre of attraction was a young soldier by the name of Fatteh. His story was that he had come from a place called Dhading, with his friend Bir Bahadur or rather Aite. After reaching Kathmandu the two had become separated and had gone their different ways.

Fatteh had gone with his pensioner recruiter. The first leg of the journey from Kathmandu had been to Nautanwa. He was then given a ticket and took the evening train, which reached the following morning at Kunraghat. Though he was hungry and tired, Fatteh's first action was to go to the depot and get his name entered in the army register. He was literally famished when he managed to finally get a good meal at one of the tea-stalls, and then the short back and sides haircut of the army plus a general cleaning up of the layer upon layer of dirt which he had accumulated on his body during the course of his travels. Fatteh passed both his general fitness and medical test. Then the getting into the new uniform, and finally the train journey to the Regimental Training Centre. Very soon after his training had been completed, he had been sent off in September 1941 to Port Swettenham in Malaya. There had been fighting and more fighting but somehow or other the Japanese had pushed the Gurkhas back towards the tip of Malaya and the sea beyond. The Gurkhas last hopes had been dashed to the ground when the expected stand at Singapore had fizzled out. The brunt of the onslaught had been met by the Australians. These particular troops, though hefty in size, were raw youngsters, and were no match for the pint-sized but formidable members of the Japanese Imperial Army, As they retreated, so did the Indian troops all along Jurong Road towards Singapore proper.

The Japanese pursued them on two levels— from the air with their fighter planes and on land with their enthusiastic ground forces.

The next stage was the ignominy of being taken prisoner. In fact all that remained of Fatteh's original battalion was just about a quarter. Some of this group, it was rumoured, had been sent to make the railroad that was being built from Bangkok to Moulmein. Most of the prisoners in this unfortunate batch met their end due to malnutrition, dysentery, malaria and finally the scourge cholera.

Subedar Fatteh was fortunate in not being in that group. In the POW camp there appeared cases of beri-beri — both the wet and dry forms. In the 'dry' form of the disease all those who were afflicted were complaining of burning hands and feet, some so much that they started dancing, or even immersing their feet in cold water, saying as they did so that their feet were 'happy'. Some of the prisoners were afflicted with the other form, where there was gradual oedema, starting with the legs and moving upwards, towards the face. The weight increased, the tissues became water–logged and ultimately the heart packed up, as life ran out in this 'wet' form' of beri beri. It was saddening to think that the cause of this somewhat grave disease was a simple lack of one of the vitamins.

It was during his days at the camp that Fatteh heard in the summer of 1943 that the Japanese controlled South-East Asia. This meant that according to the Japanese claims, they were the new masters from Burma to Malaya, the Philippines and the Dutch East Indies. The POWS (or the prisoners of war) did not believe it when the guards boasted that only Midway Island with its U.S. base remained between them and Pearl Harbour, because they had already heard rumours of the end of the war at the POW camp, and considered they were now finally free from its ill effects.

Hearing that Major Dambar Shah was with the Kalibahadurs, Fatteh enquired from him about the whereabouts of Bir Bahadur. Fatteh was sad, to hear that Bir Bahadur had probably been killed during the course of the retreat to Yaingangpokpi. The party was a great success in the sense that it brought the two groups of soldiers together. After all, their common heritage was from Nepal.

Sometime during the day they were taken on various tours of London. They saw half destroyed houses, the cracked or broken dirty window panes and some occasional craters in the ground. It would take a lot of planning and effort to put things right. Would London be built like the American cities, all laid out properly, and of such a manner that if you saw one then you had virtually seen them all ? Or would they rebuild the old London as they did following the Great Fire in 1666 ? That was the big question.

Then the gradual disperal and return – the Kalibahadurs to Kathmandu and the others to India. When Fatteh went back to India after the Victory Parade, he was a Subedar Major. This was because of the mutual understanding that the British had with the

Nepalese authorities as to the highest commission that an ordinary Nepalese would be able to hold in the Indian Brigade of Gurkhas. Now that the British were on their last legs, things were different. It was the time of pre–independence India; and Fatteh, together with his friends, had their hands full. Although Hindu-Muslim riots took place in many parts in India, it was in Calcutta that Fatteh was involved. Initially it was mass killings of the Hindus in the locality of Calcutta known as Dharmatala that started it all. After two days of mass killings by the Muslims, the Hindus started fighting back. There were the Muslims, with cries of Allah and blowing bugles as they started each offensive. The Hindus retaliated with cries of Jai Shankar and blowing of conch shells. The Sikhs, involved as a group for the Hindus, started for the Muslims with their Kirpans and created havoc. It was they and the Hindus from Bihar who saved the actual day. The Gurkhas were invoked for they were thought to be neutral and would be able to control the mischief. This was a wrong surmise, but by the time it was realised that the Gurkhas were in favour of the Hindus, at least half of Bengal had been saved for India. The horrific scenes of dead bodies piled up overnight on many lawns of Calcutta still sent shivers down the spine of Fatteh.

Then the final days and the option of which battalions of the Indian Brigade wanted to stay with the Indian Army and which within the British one. Fatteh's battalion opted to stay British ! This decision created a certain amount of disappointment at one stage when many realised that the British, because they were leaving soon, gave quick promotions to quite a few men who would soon belong to the Indian Gurkhas. Fatteh felt sore about it and swore that he would think of some way to get around the situation.

Fatteh's battalion was now in the British Gurkhas. Then he went on to Malaya with them. About a year later his Chief C.O. Campbell came to Nepal. Before Campbell had set out, Fatteh requested him to go to Dhading and meet his folks. C.O.

Campbell went to Deurali Chetrafal in Dhading district. There was a great welcome with Damai (Panch) baja and then a great reception. They even let the C.O. see the chopping off with a single stroke of the khukri, the head of the mountain goat. It was but natural in the circumstances that the goat meat was the main course of the feast. After all Fatteh's father was a man of means. Then his parents had taken C.O. Campbell to Pokhara and then to Jomsom on a sort of conducted tour. When Campbell returned from his trip to the then mysterious Nepal, it was obvious that Fatteh was slated for quick promotion. Fatteh almost certainly had a meteoric rise. Who said that personal contacts did not matter in the army ?

5

It was just after the war that Bir decided to visit Nepal. He came by steamer to Calcutta, and then from there by the land route to Kathmandu. The rubies and other stones that he had brought as a sample consignment had a quick sale in Calcutta, and as a result he had quite some money jangling in his pocket when he arrived at Kathmandu. Kathmandu was a hub of activity, for the then Prime Minister Juddha Shumsher was leaving Kathmandu soon, and going into retirement. From the news that he had heard from Nepalese expatriates at Calcutta, Bir Bahadur was under the impression that the Prime Ministership of Padma Shumsher would herald the introduction of parliamentary democracy in Nepal. The day that he arrived he heard that the next day was to be a holiday, because Maharaja Juddha Shumsher was going to take off his Shreepech or head gear and put it on Padma Shumsher's head. There were crowds in the streets when the new Maharaja rode in state on a four-horse drawn carriage around the town.

The next day Bir Bahadur started towards the village of Deurali Chetrafal, in Dhading. He went through the town, and went to pay his respects to the big stupa of Buddha at the hillock, known as Shimbhu. From there he went due west to a place called Sitapaila. There on the massive stone were what appeared to be the foot-prints of a little girl. Story had it that these were the footprints of Sita, the consort of Lord Rama. Bir Bahadur, though a Buddhist, nevertheless paid his respects at this place by picking up a little vermillion from the shrine on his finger, and applying the tika on his own forehead, and then placing a few flowers on his head. He went on from there through the paddy fields and then arrived at the bottom of a hill. There right at the top was Bhim Dhunga, and to show where he had to reach, there was a big tree, a natural land mark for miles around.

Climbing up the slope with him were quite a few people, all Nepalese. Most it seemed, were going to the temple of Mankamana (Wish Come True temple) There were however some traders taking various goods up to Pokhara, even beyond. Bir found some companions, and talking with them, he climbed the mountain leisurely. From the top the progress was rather rapid for it was all the way downhill—the Thadodando—the trouble with this place will be on the return journey, thought Bir. Then the journey on the flat, and reaching Deurali, the place from where he and Chandra had as children see the great earthquake of 1934. Then the journey throught the village, and the descent down the hillside to that projection known as Moktan's Hill. It brought back vivid memories in Bir's mind. The place looked almost the same except for the fact that the Sallaghari of pine trees looked a bit thinner.

As Bir walked to the place, a few of the people recognised him but most did not. After all, it had been a good seven years since he had been away. As he reached the porch of the house he saw a man sitting in front of it and sharpening a scythe. The man looked up and started at Bir. Bir in turn was taken a little aback, for the man was rather dark complexioned and haggard. Could this be his brother ? In a more or less querulous tone, Bir uttered "Chandra ?" whereupon the latter stood up with recognition in his eyes.

Dropping the scythe to the ground Chandra rushed forward towards Bir, saying, "At last you have come back. How I have been looking forward to this day ! Father is ill and on his last legs. I am ill, and it is quite a strain on mother. Chameli does come occasionally to help but she has her own house to look after."

Bir entered the dark ground floor of the house. It was

no longer an animal shed, for there was a bed in one corner which was presumably Chandra's. Up the stairs and, there was his father Hari Bahadur. He looked frail and certainly on his last legs. His mother told him that they had brought the jhankri, and got him to drive away a few spirits, but it was of no avail. Bir was rather shocked at this state of affairs and suggested that they should all set out for Kathmandu and Bir Hospital.

"Don't bother about me, Bir. I am an old man now, and have not got many days left. Talk to Chandra of going to Kathmandu, and getting himself cured. After all, he has to get married and settle down. He has to produce children—sons I mean to continue on our line. But forget about us: tell me all that has happened to you since you went away. To tell you the truth, I never expected that the day would dawn when I would set my eyes on you again Bir," said Hari Bahadur.

'It's a long story, but I will tell you just some of the main points right now. I can tell you all the details over the next few weeks that I am going to be here. As you know Fatteh and myself set out from here and went to Kathmandu. We got separated there for Fatteh went to join the Indian Brigade of Gurkhas whilst I went to join the Nepalese Army and the Kalibahadurs. After some training in Kathmandu we were taken to Kabul in India and then from there to Peshawar. Following the news of the Allies setback at Dunkirk, we were sent to Manipur and then to the meeting with the Japanese. We fought like hell there. There was no question of fleeing from that bloody battle, for it would have meant that we would be caged like prisoners. Can you imagine something like that happening to the Gurkhas. Anyway we fought like hell but had to retreat, and when we broke up to retreat that was the time that I was picked up by the Japs. They were taking me either to be shot, or to one of their POW campus. I fled into the jungle and into a Burmese village.'

"Now that you are back are you going to join the

Kalibahadurs again ?" asked Hari Bahadur.

"I suppose I ought to go and report there, but I will give it a few days yet," said Bir knowing full well that he had no intention of doing that. In fact coming to Nepal he had lied, saying that he was a chowkidar in Calcutta, and had come home on leave.

"Yes you must, my son, go back to the Kalibahadurs."

"I was in that village most of the war for there was no real possibility of my rejoining my regiment. The real fact was that not only the Kalibahadurs but also the rest of the Gurkhas in Burma had been called back. The Windgate Expedition, with its hit and run tactics was treated no differently, and it too was recalled. Until the actual bombing of Nagasaki and Hiroshima, it was the Japanese who had a full day. I could do nothing but lie low. At that time I heard that at a place called Moguk, which was just across the river Irrawaddy and to the East, there were plenty of rubies for the taking. As soon as the war was over I went there for I had heard fabulous tales of the treasures to be found. When I got there I found this to be true and in fact this area seemed to be wholly reserved for the British and Gurkhas and a handful of Indians. I met and made friends with a few Gurkhas there and worked as a loader in mines. During this last couple of years, I managed to get a license from the British Govt. and as a license holder was allowed to dig. and what I found was mine. I managed to make a hoard of rubies, and this I am in the process of selling. Let us say I am making a market or least looking for one."

Old Hari Bahadur nodded. He was happy with the thought that his son would now be able to stand on his own legs either within or out of the army. He did not make any comment as to what to do in the future.

During the first week there, Bir met a young girl called Sunu Maya Thokar. He made friends with her and then as the relationship grew he found that he was in love with her. The secret furtive meetings continued and the flames of passions being roused it was no surprise that the two started slipping into the woods daily for the explicit purpose of ilicit union. After the second week Bir thought that he would like to get married to Sunu Maya and he spoke to his father about it. Hari Bahadur said it was out of the question for Sunu Maya Thokar to marry him, Bir Bahadur, a Moktan, as they were of Mith–thars, or blood–cousins. Hearing this from his father, Bir did not confide his troubles either to his brother Chandra or to Tilak Bahadur Thokar, who was Sunu Maya's father.

Two weeks of stay at Deurali, Chetrafal was enough for Bir Bahadur. One day after their secretive union in the jungle he turned to Sanu Maya and asked her if she would be willing to go with him to Calcutta and then Burma.

Sunu Maya thought for a while and then replied, "Going to Calcutta is alright with me but then what happens after that. I don't think that you will be able to get me to Burma. Come to think of it, I don't think you will be able to get me out of Nepal. You know that young girls are not allowed out of the country except with a special permit. You don't have that, nor are you entittled to get one for me."

"A permit may be necessary but I can get that quite easily. I will only have to spend a little more money, that's all."

"That's all right, Bir, but the big question is what you will do with me at Calcutta. Once you get there and then have to move on, you will leave me. I can't come back to this village for I will not be able to show my face. There will be no way of supporting myself, and to earn a living I might have to resort to prostitution!"

Bir made an expression of surprise and was about to say something in protest but Sunu Maya continued, "No, No. Don't look surprised. It is what most Lahure dais do They take a girl from the village to some city in India such as Calcutta or Bombay, with big promises of highly paid jobs and then leave them there. I know all this for only the other day they arrested a man called

Man Bahadur Tamang from Nuwakot. What guarantee is there that this won't come to pass to me?"

Bir did not make any further attempt to argue. Her mind was made up, he felt. Sunu Maya was not going to leave Chetrafal come what may. The next day, before it was quite light, Bir called his brother Chandra, and giving him Re 3,000 for day to day expenses, he left the house for the second time. There were no good-byes to his parents, for Bir felt that they might not be able to bear this second parting at this stage of their lives. Well, for Sunu Maya, he would have to try to forget her. She could not marry him, she was not prepared to come with him, nor in fact to trust him as he would have expected her to do. It had been nice knowing her, and he must try to come back to see her some day.

When Bir got back to Calcutta. He decided to live it up for quite a few days. He met a few of the Nepalese there, and had offers to join the so-called liberation force that was being formed. Bir promised that he would think about it and would also convey the news to a number of the Nepalese who were in the 'Burrifs' or the Burma Rifles or to those who were in the police force. Bir made a number of contacts, exchanged a few addresses, and then decided to make preparation for the return journey to Burma.

It was his night prowlings along the Red Light districts of Calcutta that convinced him that it was not the Anglo-Indian, or Indian girls who were most involved in the trade. Quite a few of the girls were Nepalese and they were willing to talk to a fellow Nepalese and tell him their troubles. How they had been brought on false promises by fellow Nepalese, and how they had been let down, seemed to be the general run of their stories. Then after years of this life, what had they to look forward to ! It was nothing more than an old age of misery with many having to resort to the streets to beg. Bir, realised that Sunu Maya had been right.

This did not prevent Bir from being a regular visitor to the red-light districts, more particularly one in Chitpur road. After some days he developed some swelling in the groins and then developed a discharge from the penis. His visit to the doctor was more a dressing down for being so infected. Bir would have to undergo a course of injections, but he was fortunate, for the new wonder drug penicillin was now available in the open market. Price being no factor, it was no problem for Bir to pay Rs. 100 per day for a five days course. Bir's troubles were however not over, for no sooner had he got over his infection of syphills and gonorrhoea, than he developed an attack of mumps. Initially it was just his checks which were swollen, but when his testicles became swollen, he found that his doctor seemed rather worried. Though the doctor did not say anything to him, Bir could feel that something was amiss. But luckily the trouble was controlled.

When Bir reached back to Burma after the unexpected delay at Calcutta, he found that there was a letter waiting for him. It was from Chandra stating that his father's arghan had been fixed for Nov. 25th. It was already the 23rd and thus it was physically impossible for Bir to get back to it. He resigned himself to the situation. He thought that Chandra must have arranged it all. The first day's rites and expenses must have been borne by him. Then the expenses of the first night, and all the expenses for the 108 oil lamps and the food must be borne by Chameli, his sister. Then after that the charge would fall on Chandra again.

It was a good three months later that he received another letter from home. It was from his mother. She said that Chandra had gone to the hospital at Kathmandu for treatment. The doctors had found out that he had been suffering from Kala-azar and had instituted treatment for the disease. But God's will, Chandra had died. His mother was arranging Chandra's arghan on the forty-ninth day. Would he, Bir be able to attend.

Bir wondered what the world was coming to. Everyone

dying, first his father and now his brother. His thoughts turned towards home and naturally to Sunu Maya Thokar. He must find out what happened to her. A week went by and then the events which had seemed so large, gradually fell into its proper perspective, and Bir's thoughts turned once more to the immediate matters in hand.

+ + + +

The Burmese support for the British had been lukewarm during the early years of the war. This was more evident with the withdrawal of the British and the subsequent siding of the Burmese with the Japanese and the formation of the puppet Burmese cabinets under the Japanese umbrella. During this period the contacts with the Japanese and the activities of the Indians, more particularly those of the Azad Hind, increased greatly; but the initial enthusiasm gave way to disenchantment due to high handedness of the Japanese officials not only to the population at large, but also to the monks; and also due to the harsh brutality meted out to all by the military police known as Kempeitai. In the end the Burmese army and the Azad Hind forces both turned against the Japanese, for they realised that the Japanese had come not as liberators, but as masters, and that after all, the independence of Burma, as well as India, was at stake.

The end of the war meant a Burmese government under a British Governor, and it was obvious soon enough that though the British were not initially keen to let go of their colonies, it was nevertheless the hard realities of the situation that made them give independence to India, Pakistan, Ceylon and also Burma. When Burma became independent and a Republic in 1946, the new government took, at the same time, the then rather unusual step of leaving the Commonwealth. This act of severing all ties with the immediate past did lead to some initial difficulties.

Till the time that the British handed over the reins of government, things had been quiet and independence had been achieved more or less peaceably. This lull before the actual storm lasted barely two months. With the second and final withdrawal of the British in the eventful decade, there were, however, considerable upheavals in various parts of the country. This had been partly expected, for what had been Burma under the British had been a great conglomeration of religions, languages, tribes and political thoughts. It was putting it very simply when one stated that there were seven states with nine major tribes, and that most of the people were Buddhists with as much as twenty percent being Muslims. When one delved more deeply, one realised how incomplete this statement was; for Shan State, for example, comprised infact of a lot of different units, each with its own chief or Raja.

The occurence of a series of revolts in different parts of the country that independence created in Burma was now followed by civil war. There was a great hotch-potch of these fighters—not one, but two groups of Reds were involved — the Red Flag Communists and the White Flag Communists, together with the Karen tribesmen, the Mon tribesmen, the Mujahid Muslims, and a marauding army of Koumintang Chinese soldiers who had been driven across the border from China. The influx of such Chinese did not however make much impact on the overall population of Burma. Even the people's Volunteer Organisation was split into the Yellow and White Bands—one for and one against the government. The fact that at one stage of this upheaval, the government controlled little more than Rangoon city was probably just due to its fortunate location on the Rangoon river at a point some twenty miles from the sea. A little more push by the rebels aided by the First, and some men of the Third Burma Rifles, and the government in Rangoon would have been driven into the sea. In the wake of this, were the strikes by the civil servants and the railway workers. Things were grinding to a halt: but on another front there was hectic activity. There were daylight robberies in Rangoon and a similar state of affairs existed at Mandalay soon after its fall to the rebels. Slowly but surely however, and in course of time, the various rebellions were supressed and the country had some form of law and order; but only when the military had, at least, flexed its muscles.

+ + + +

When Bir returned to Burma, he found that the independence of the country had had some effect even in Moguk. Bir was still a licence holder, albeit he had now to have it renewed periodically. Now of course, besides the English, Indians and Gurkhas, there were also about one to two percent of the locals who were engaged in the ruby trade. After getting the licence, one dug and sieved through the gravel, and then it was a case of 'finders keepers'. Bir and the others engaged in this trade did not have to worry as in the days of yore, when all the rubies over a certain weight had to be handed over. Of course, there were ways of getting around it, as by breaking up the stones into smaller ones, but the net result of all this was that no real sparklers were generally handed over.

Bir had worked as a loader in one of the British owned ruby mines. Now however he took out a licence and said that he was also digging for rubies in the usual primitive manner. The idea of this was two-fold. His work as a loader of gravel gave him access to information about new finds. Some of his friends then used to smuggle these out, and lo behold ! it would be refound by Bir or in his indigenously run mine. This could sell openly. Some of the other smuggled out stones had to be got out of Burma and this they did by putting the stones in a fermented form of salted and pressed fish paste called 'ngapi', a popular condiment eaten with rice and curry. Another alternative was also in a fish preparation called 'balachow', which was basically shrimps, onions, tomatoes etc which had been fried or even mixed with something else. In course of time however, the authorities got a little wise to these capers and so the export of both 'ngapi' or 'balachow' was not allowed, or was at least highly suspected as covers for gems.

Moguk, some distance north of Mandalay and with the hills all surrounding it, was highly reminescent of Kathmandu. Not only this, but the cultivation in those hills was in the fashion of the terraced fields of Nepal. The houses were also similar to the small cottages of the hills of Nepal—white structures with thatched roofs and with the red clay splattered not only on the floor inside but also on the frontage of the house itself. There were also the millet cobs and the garlic bulbs hanging in clusters around the window frame and under the eaves of the cottage roof. Except for those engaged in the mining, quite a substantial percentage of the people were farmers involved in the dairy industry and supplying milk and ghee to the rest.

The Nepali community itself was like its counterpart in the Nepali hills— the women folk with their big dhungris on their ears and bulakis on their nostrils. These were simple folk, who even went to the cinema screen to do darshan, when any Indian film with a religious background was showing at the local hall.

It was then whilst working at these ruby mines at Moguk that Bir met his wife to be. She was a girl of the Shan tribe and Bir wooed and won her hand. He was happy for after these many years in Burma, Bir realised that the Shan mentality, in comparison to that of the other tribes, was much more compatible to his. The Shans were a soft-spoken and polite people who made it a point to be kind and considerate to their contacts.

The leader of the Nepali speaking community there was a man who had been in Burma for a good forty years. He was respected and loved by all and because of his beard was referred to as Mahila Dai. The big question then, during the rule of Prime Minister U. Nu, was whether the Nepalese community should opt for Burmese citizenship. and quite a few did do it. Some even went to the extent of Burmisation of their names, hoping that this would naturally lead to their getting some sort of preferential treatment. Most of the people of Nepali origin however preferred to retain their names and get a Foreign Registration Certificate (F.R.C.) with its added headaches.

Money was coming in quite well and life for Bir and his wife was not bad at all. They had their own house in the suburb of Mogok. It was a small house made completely out of wood and raised on piles above the ground. Bir was in the enviable position of even being able to send money home. Although he could have at that time sent upto Rs 600 per month. he just sent Rs. 100 to his mother and Rs. 50 to his sister Chameli.

Bir Bahadur and his wife Way Shin Yi wanted to have children but in spite of their continuous attempts, Way Shin Yi did not become pregnant. Bir secretly wondered whether it was the syphilis or the gonorrhoea infections that he had picked up at Calcutta which was the cause of this. He was virtually sure that the mumps attack, during which he had had some swelling of the testicles did not have much to do with it. He took his wife to the Burmese doctors, the medicine men and finally to the 'weza' or wise men. The various charms or amulets that they suggested seemed of no avail. Manipuri astrologers or Brahmin palmistry experts known as 'Punna', who were as far away as Mandalay were visited in the hope that they would forecast the future. The experts were partly right as far as Bir and Way Shin Yi's commercial venture was concerned, but their predictions about future births in the family all went haywire. The couple's business prospered partly because of Way Shin Yi's sound instincts as far as money matters were concerned. It was true that she did spend a fair amount of money in religious works or worship but this was purely from a self interest which was partly for the birth of a child and partly to ensure that she and Bir would be credited with merit for the salvation of their souls in the hereafter.

6

The prospect of fighting as mercenaries for the cause of delivering Nepal from the feudal rule of the Ranas became a very attractive proposition to a good many of the Nepalese who were in Burma during these troubled days. Quite a few had their own arms and some stock of ammunition. These had been a legacy of the retreating British and the Japanese armies, a remnent from the days of the underground fight against the Japanese, and was a precious possession which had been wisely and secretly hidden for possible use in the future. Now the time had arrived when it would pay good dividends. With this in mind, quite a few of the retired or even active members of the Nepalese community in Burma set out for Calcutta. They headed for a place referred to in layman's parlance as Nepal House, on Chowringhee.

There was a good deal of cameraderie at what had formerly been the building of one of the famous departmental stores of Calcutta. When the British left the shores of India for good, they had as a sign of goodwill given it to a Nepalese at what had been a give-away price. After a couple of years, during which time dust had settled all over the place, there was a sudden hum of activity. There were people coming and going, bringing news or taking things out from this place referred to by all, as Nepal House. The first set back, it seemed was greeted with a mood of depression all around. This was because of the news that a certain Dil. Bahadur Rai, who had been sent to Kathmandu in September of 1950, had been caught by the Nepal government intelligence, and had confessed that he was the harbinger of cache of arms in a plan to equip and arm to the teeth men in no less than seven different places in Nepal. With such stimultaneous ernption at different places, the idea was to create a diversion in all directions, to provide a camouflage for the actual object of rescuing King Tribhuvan from the cluthes of the Ranas. The headline news on his arrest in all the Calcutta papers brought to focus their centre of activity at Chowringhee Road. The only unknown fact initially was whether Dil Bahadur Rai had been actually caught or whether he had been bought over the Ranas. Everyone was on edge at Nepal House and a system of code words, identity cards and limitations were enforced to forestall any sort of retaliation or attack by persons on the Rana payroll.

It was on November 6, in 1950, that King Tribhuvan and virtually the whole of the Royal Family took refugee in the grounds of the then Indian Embassy at Sital Niwas. This was a bomb-shell, for such an occurence had never taken place in the annals of Nepal. The flight into India by King Tribhuvan from Gauchar Airport some four days later meant that events were moving fast —events which in the course of the next hundred days would see his return as the head of a domestic set-up in Nepal.

The Revolution had begun, and news of its imminence were heralded when during the course of one night an aircraft of a commercial airways flew over the valley of Kathmandu and scattered leaflets all over the place. By this time Bir Bahadur and a few hundreds of his comrades had already reached the borders of Nepal and during the course of one night had by setting off a few rounds of ammunition, plus it is said pyrotechnic bombs had managed to capture the Bada Hakim at Birgunj. Bir Bahadur and other volunteers of the Nepali Congress were now the forces of the Mukti Sena or the Liberation Forces. Fighting took place not only at Birgunj, when it changed hands again but also in various parts of the country. Revolts took place in places as far apart as Biratnagar, Okhaldhunga, Dhankuta and Kailali-Kanch-anpur. It was no longer a simple localised affair.

With the lack of British support to the Rana regime, it was apparent that its days were numbered. The countdown was in force from that fateful day in November. Fighting was spreading to other parts of the country. With the return of the King to Nepal, one further chapter in its history had ended. The Mukti Sena became an anachronism and were soon converted into what came to be known as the Raksha Dal, or defence forces. Bir Bahadur was happy now, for after all, he was back in Nepal, not as an ordinary citizen but as one who had had an active role in freeing Nepal from the feudal Ranas. To him it seemed so incomprehensible that 104 years of Rana rule should have crumbled to dust in almost just the same number of days.

A few months were to pass. They were months of adulation for all the members of the Raksha Dal. This applied more so to the Officers for it was they who were invited and feted at the recently opened hotels of Kathmandu. This new found freedom was something to which the Nepalese were unused. The round of parties, dinners and cabarets were the order of the day; the day to day occurences, a massive round of parties if ever there was one. The trouble with all this was that one met the same set of people from one party to another. After all Kathmandu was small, the elite were as a group smaller, and those involved in these daily rounds of parties were fewer still. There were also bars with exotic names such as 'Rendezvous Bar', 'Purnima Night' and 'The Little Room'. Not only that but for the specially favoured customers there was invariably a special room at the back where one could indulge in, or watch a strip-tease in private.

All this had its advantages, for Bir in course of a few parties developed an attachment to a young girl called Sheila. He never bothered to find out what her surname was. They would meet at the parties at some massive house, usually called some palace or the other. There was the usual dancing and then after a certain interval of time there was the 'lights-off' and by this time partners had been selected. Sometimes there was partner swapping, but most of the time Bir fouud that he was invariably with Sheila. Why he had no serious competitors for her he did not know. Perhaps it was because of his young and manly age of twenty-seven combined with his physique, which created an attraction in Sheila's mind for him. He was certain of it that Sheila preferred him to many of the foggy old men who were at these parties. Then after the parties, she usually accompanied him to his lodgings but she always made it a point to leave the house early in the morning before the inhabitants of the town were up.

The centre of their activity or Bir Bahadur's lodging was in fact a house in which some of the officers of the Raksha Dal were billeted. In was a house with two gables and was appropriately called 'Dui Burja'. The house was in itself strategically placed for it was just outside the compound of the Singha Durbar but because there was a small gate in the compound wall, it meant that access to it was easy.

Story had it that this was a sort of sanatorium for the ladies of Chandra Shumsher's household when he was Prime Minister of the country. Was it just a sanatorium for the ill or was it a place where those who had fallen out of favour found themselves in, was what Bir thought. The first day the Mukti Sena had taken over the house, they had found some of the ladies, dainty figures like the lilies in the pond, in front of the house. Bir was not convinced that the ladies moved out of the house when his comrades moved in. If they did move out it was just a temporary affair, for they were now flirting in and out like Bir's own friend Sheila. It made him laugh just to think about it. How hypocrital was Sheila's usual practice of collecting some flowers from the garden with the idea that anyone seeing her with these floral items would think that she was on the way to some temple, and perhaps of how devout a young lady she was.

Like the old story of the two male tigers being unable to live in the same cage, it was but natural that things should come to a head at some time. There were not just two but many tigers. A few months after the liberation, it so happened that a group of athparias went to the local prison where their leader was held and managed to set him free. They then set about brandishing the khukuris, and it looked at one time if there would be a three cornered contest with the Khukuri Dal athparias, the Raksha Dal and the Army in the three corners of an equilateral triangle. This episode turned out to be no more than a storm in a tea cup and things looked calm at first glance.

The inner tensions prevailed and though the officers of Raksha Dal such as Bir Bahadur were quite happy with the existing arrangements, it was not so for the general rank and file. Some started taking things into their own hands and in course of time, the local populace started referring to them as the Rakchesh Dal, though never to their faces. Though never directly claimed or stated it was an open secret that there was deep hostility between the regular army and the Raksha Dal. These elements, such as Bir Bahadur were prabashis who had come from Burma, Sikkim, Assam and Bengal to see what they could get out of the whole episode, to see if there was anything to be picked up.

One day Bir Bahadur was thinking all these thoughts, and saying them to Sheila, when she turned to him and said, "From what you have told me of your life, why don't you go to Deurali Chetrafal in Dhading and meet your mother and sister. They must be pining for news of you, for after all, one's kin is one's kin."

"I know that you are right. I must go and meet my mother. She must be grief-stricken following the death of the old man as well as poor Chandra. I wonder if Chameli has been able to come to comfort her. It must be pretty hard on mother in her old age. I have to ask for leave to go to Dhading." As he uttered these words his thoughts turned to Sunu Maya. His thoughts turned to remorse. How he had he forgotten her just like that ? Would he also forget Sheila just like that in a period of time ? He wondered. Was there something basically wrong with him as a man ? Had he no roots at all ? Was he after all just a rolling stone and no more?

That visit to Dhading was not to be at that moment. Bir Bahadur was in charge of the garrison that was at Singha Durbar and they were there to guard a leader who had been recently charged with leading an uprising. The funny things was, this leader was one of them, a person who Bir Bahadur knew very well.

On a cold dark night in January 1952, the first indication that something was amiss was when the electricity failed and the telephone went out of order. Various groups of the Raksha Dal, Bir Bahadur among them, were then deputed to various parts of the town. The prisons. the radio-station, the wireless, the telephone office, soon fell under the control of the Raksha Dal. With various groups dispatched to various places Bir Bahadur came back to Singha Durbar and took his position on one of the rooms over the massive gate supports. He would guard the stronghold with a Sten gun and Lord pity anyone who came to rush him. A coup d' etat had been attempted, and it was now a question of do or die'.

There were others also in that room. Before it got light one of them, a certain Dan Bahadur said, "There should be someone from the Army going to the Dharahara and giving a bugle call. This is the usual signal for all troops to assemble on the Tundikhel at any time of crisis. After all it seems that all of the government is now in the palace. We have got them where we want them."

Bir Bahadur digested this information. He was unused to the ways of Kathmandu but this complacency on the part of Dan Bahadur seemed rather odd to him. After all there were the palace guards and they would surely offer some resistance if the Raksha Dal tried to storm the palace itself.

It got light, but still no emergency bugle. It fact when the morning bugle sounded at 6.00 a.m. there was no sign whatsoever that anything was amiss. What Bir Bahadur, with powerful field glasses to his eyes noticed, was that troops were collecting as usual and going from the Tundikhel, and seemed to be going in the general direction of the palace. He was sure that his old unit the Kalibahadurs plus others such as the Gorakh Bahadurs and the Mahendra Dyl were perhaps going there with all their arms ammunition. Would the army come over to the side of the Raksha Dal? Seeing all this activity in the opposite direction he doubted it. When would the show down occur ? He was'nt sure. Would it be tomorrow or the day after. That would depend on the rations that the Raksha Dal had at Singh Durbar. When this thought came to his mind he contacted his superiors and got landed with the job of procuring rations. That came for sticking his head out, thought Bir Bahadur.

By mid-day he had managed to get some provisions into Singha Durbar. It was not enough and so they went out again. This time when a group of four, under the command of Bir Bahadur had got as far as the far end of Putali Sadak, all four suddenly heard a voice say, "Go, and join the Rakchesh Dal."

All four whirled in a jiffy and pointing their guns at the direction from where the voice had come said, "Say that again." A couple of small boys, little realising that their innocent words could cause such fury to a group of soldiers with their nerves on edge, just trembled in their shoes. They stood still, unable to utter a sound. It was only when the soldiers had turned round and continued on in their mission that the boys picked up enough courage to scurry back to the safe comfort of their homes.

As the afternoon wore on, Bir Bahadur and his comrades knew that they were fighting a losing battle. Squads of the regular army, though unarmed, came and collected their arms, without a single shot being fired. It all seemed ironic to Bahadur that what had promised to be massive bang, capable of shaking the very foundations of the whole set-up was now ending in a whimper. It was a total fiasco as the leaders gave instructions that not a single shot was to be fired.

Bir Bahadur had no intention of spending his life in a

jail or, if spared, then in certain ignominy. He left his arms and ammunition within the compound of Singha Durbar and, changing into mufti he quietly slipped out of the back gate, together with a couple of friends. The next few days were arduous but he endured it, and leaving behind his un-reunited family and his new friend Sheila, he headed back to Burma and his wife there during that eventful January of 1952.

Whether the authorities were keen that he and his friends should leave the country or not, Bir was not quite sure. It seemed very easy to get away from Kathmandu on the old road through Chandra Gadhi and Bhimphedi. Perhaps the people at the various check points made it doubly sure that no obstruction was placed on their hasty journey out of the country. After reaching Raxaul, Bir Bahadur and his friends set out for Gorakhpur, and reached there in the morning at 10.00 a.m. At the station they found out that the train left at 4.00 in the evening. Some of the soldiers wanted to spend some time at Gorkhapur to let things settle at Kathmandu. There were just two others who wanted to go on to Burma. Seeing that there was still a good six hours to go before their train left, the two decided to go to town to see a movie. They left belongings in the 'Left Luggage' and saying they would be back, left Bir Bahadur to be the sole remnant of the original group at the Gorakhpur railway station, Bir got his ticket, but because he had barely Rs 1000 on him and did not have any idea of how long he might have to make it last, he was not really ready to spend it thoughtlessly. In fact it seemed that his premonition was correct, for it was nearly four O'clock and his friends had not returned from the picture, if they had really been to see one as they had said. It was more than likely they were in the arms of some ladies of leisure, he thought. He did not blame them, he wished he had gone with them. Now, however, that the ticket had been bought he decided he would continue on to Burma and his wife. Two days of travelling in the third class compartment brought him to Gauhati. Reaching there at 9.00 p.m., he found that he had more of a problem than anything else. It was much better in the third class compartment, that he had travelled in. There was, at least, the safety of numbers. On the platform here, there was no question of beds and beddings, and Bir was fearful that if he left his few possessions unguarded, or went to sleep, he might lose what little he had. He had not slept for two days. It was a little relief to him when he saw two people, and thinking these lads to be Nepali, he asked, "Are you Nepali ?"

"No, we are Manipures, and we are students· We come from Agra."

Looking at them Bir would have thought that they were Nepalese, but this did not seem to be borne out by the facts. "Well, I seem to be going in the same direction, if you are going back home. Do you mind if I stick with you ?"

The lads did not say anything, and Bir took this to mean that they had no objections. Because of the presence of these two, a Dhyan Kishore Singh and a Nikam Bodh he felt a little at ease; and as he now had kept his suitcase with theirs, and sitting by it, he just dosed off on a bench on the platform.

The train steamed out of Gauhati station the next morning at 6.00 a.m. and it was a relatively short journey for they reached Dinapur at about 2.00 p.m It seemed all quiet but the reason was quite simple: for there was a curfew on. It was now apparent to Bir that had he not had the two lads with him it would have been a really troublesome journey. For example, he found out at the bus station at Dinapur that he required a permit to go from Dinapur to Manipur. This permit said that he was a bookseller from Darjeeling and was Indian. There was some risk in this permit, for it was a permit to cross Nagaland only. Bir got the permit also because there was a 'Nepali' police officer as S.P.— a certain Inspector C.B. Lama, who issued the pass in good faith, but nevertheless warned them that there was a great danger in going to Nagaland.

The next day they travelled by the Manipur Road Transport corporation bus to Manipur. The nearly 200 kilometres trip took almost seven hours. The road from Dinapur to Manipur or Imphal was cut out in the hillsides and had a lot of turns and hairpin bends. Somewhere along the middle of this road, after traversing a big slope was the town of Kohima on the top of a hill – this place was probably as big as Kathmandu and as beautiful as Darjeeling. A truly beautiful place, fit to be the capital of any state. The most important check-post was as they neared Imphal or Manipur. There was also a certain amount of inconvenience due to the army/police checks at no less than three places. The checks were however routine but the presence of the Manipur lads was again a blessing. They reached Imphal at about three in the afternoon and it was only after taking Bir to the local dharmashala, and fixing up a room for him that the lads went off to their own homes.

Left to his own thoughts, Bir reviewed all that had happened so as to change his life. The eventful journey from Nepal and his fortunate encounter with the lads. Had they only spoken Nepali they could have passed themselves off as his countrymen, there was so much similarity in the facial expressions. And though they were Indians they did not seem to like the Indians. Bir, himself a Nepali, though now having spent so many years in Burma had reciprocal feelings. Was it because the Nepalese were never thankful as a race? Was it because of the 'we know it all' or 'Big Brother' attitude adopted by the Indians? Was the attitude of the Nepalese towards the Indians similar to that of the Irish to the English ? Enjoying most of the benefits of a liaison, but always ready to slap their faces if the occasion demanded or offered.

Imphal was almost like Kathmandu, not only just the hills all around but also the weather was similar. The people of Imphal, or Manipur as some called it, all seemed to have Mongolian type of features. Bir rested at the Marbari dharmasala for it was quite a nice place and went around the town a little later in the afternoon. The next day Bir travelled from Imphal to Moreh.

The road was 95 kilometres of frightening mountain road, and it took a good nine hours to traverse. The anxiety that the bus might topple over the side of the mountain, was increased by the thought that the Nagas might come around the corner any time and make an attack. If they did, the two sentries with their guns, who were also travelling in the bus could hardly have been any match. The passengers in the bus, the ones who usually travelled to and fro seemed quite at ease; and so Bir too decided that 'What will be,' and rested on his seat. Bir reached the place at three in the afternoon and from there Burma was barely thirty minutes walk on foot. Thence forward across the border into Burma, to Tambhu and from there to Maymyo near Mandalay, a six day journey on foot. Maymyo, the previous capital of Burma was where his wife was.

Maymyo was a little Nepal, for there was the Gorkha Road to remind everyone about it. Not only that, even the other Burmese traders could speak a smattering of Nepali to the shoppers strolling in the market. Bir's wife Way Shin Yi was staying there with some relatives of hers.

The most important change now was of course the Foreigners Registration Certificate or F.R.C. and Bir had to either opt for that or apply for a National Registration Certificate. It was fortunately the time of U. Nu and it was not difficult for people of Nepalese origin to get a N.R.C.

The bigger change was yet to come. Whereas, formerly, the people of the Nepali community used to greet each other with 'Jai Nepal' it was now more awkward to do so. Then Bir found that he was not the only one of the mercenaries who had returned from Nepal. There were lots of others. These people who were a class above the poorer people of Nepalese descent, gradually created the impression that it was no longer appropriate with the changed circumstances in Nepal to retain the Gurkha name. This led to faction formation and what had been one body for the whole community before now became the Gorkha Sangha and the

Nepali Sangh. The poorer section of the community being in the Gorkha Sangh; it was no wonder that this was the one which ultimately lost in the fray. But the community did not have major problems. They could on payment of twelve kyats per year still get their little 'Black Book' and also their identity cards to come to Nepal and get subsequent Nepalese citizenship.

7

With the flourishing of the ruby business, Bir Bahadur had made enough to be able to afford a holiday. It was also partly to pacify his wife, whose other interest beside the business, was religion. It was understandable to Bir that she was a little sad because she had no children. She herself seemed very conscious of her barrenness, although no one had referred to her as 'amyunma'.

It was the daily habit of Way Shin Yi to visit all the Buddhist pagodas at Mogok. When she gave alms to the procession of yellow-robed Buddhist 'pongi or rahans' viz the priests or monks, she made her feelings known. They nodded and said that perhaps she should visit the Buddhist shrines of Rangoon and Mandalay, then further afield as, to India, Nepal and perhaps even Ceylon. Her duty was to venerate the doctrine of the Buddha and she would be surely rewarded.

The last few years had seen a lot of happenings in Burma. Bir and Way Shin Yi had heard or seen all these happenings. First of all there was the building of the World Peace Pagoda, a product of the brain of U. Nu. The building of this, some eight miles north of Rangoon, and the holding of the Buddhist Conference there were matters which were dear to the heart of U. Nu. This Sixth Buddhist Synod was a grave attempt on the part of U. Nu to try to start a dialogue and bring together to some extent the Hinayana and the Mahayana schools of Buddhism. He was partly successful in this but it was up to the future generations to judge this. To achieve rapport with the surrounding countries he even had a peepal tree flown over from Kasi or Varanasi and planted in the precincts of the Shwedagon pagoda. At the same time he also had constructed in the same precincts a rectangular 'pillar', tapering towards the top and had on it sculpturing to show the whole life of the Buddha.

The Nepalese Community at Rangoon also rose to the occasion and decided to construct a Nepalese Mandir in this area. Nestled in one corner of this vast comples, it was a simple modest shed like structure. What however made it different was that one side of the shed rose upwards to form two tiers of a pagoda like structure. As one went in through the side door, one could at once detect the Nepalese influence, for the centre of attraction was modern: a sculptor's concept of, some said Annapurna, and some said Gaurishankar. Whichever one it was, this green mountain like structures had a number of niches built in it. There were also four stupa like structures, the biggest being at the very top. The infiuence of Hinduism was apparent; one realised that one of the two figures was that of Narad, or Mahana Saikala as the Burmese call him. Besides this, there were pictures of Durga, Ganesh, Shivaji, Saraswati and Indra in Burmese dress plus the usual pictures of Krishna. An unusual feature was, however, some still other pictures which depicted the type of person that one was expected to be in relation to the day of the week on which one was born.

Then came the epoch making year of 1956 – the 2,500th anniversary of the Birth, attainment of Enlightenment and attainment of Nirvana of Buddha. This was the time which, according to the Tharavade Buddhist reckoning, would herald the period of world peace. This was too the year of the Fourth World Buddhist Conference, when King Mahendra, taking personal interest in the development of Lumbini not only visited Buddha's birth place but also donated funds for its development.

These years of U. Nu's premiership, before he resigned, were the hey day of Burma and Nepal friendship. Burma, though in economic difficulties herself had offered scholarships to Nepalese students to study medicine and other courses there. The colourful premier, the once 'Tartay – Saturday's Son', but now an ardent Buddhist, had offered to help finance the development of Lumbini as a place of Buddhist pilgrimage. Would the Seventh Buddhist Synod be held at Lumbini, in Nepal wondered both Bir and Way Shin Yi?

Bir felt that it was now the appropriate time to show Way Shin Yi what had been his homeland before he set out for Burma. Rangoon was, therefore literally the first port on an eventful pilgrimage. It was also natural that the first place of visit on this journey was to the famed Shwedagon Pagoda at Rangoon. They went up the slope and thence went barefooted to the lift, and in a jiffy were up to the long covered walk towards the pagoda. Looking back at the lift which was once again hurtling downwards to bring up more worshippers, they realised that from this vantage point they could see in the distance, the various ships at the Rangoon harbour. As they walked on, they passed the various boxed in inscriptions on the walls, denoting the various amounts that the persons concerned had donated for the pagoda. How characteristic of the Burmese trait, to give to religious centres or causes. Inside this complex, the first place to which Bir took his wife was the building at the foot of the pagoda, to pay homage to three Noble Gems viz. the Buddha, the Law and the Assembly. Then to the relics of the Buddha. Both husband of wife knelt before the iron grilled door, with the two massive images on either side and prayed silently to the Lord.

Bir knew all the important areas of the pagoda complex. He started at the Nepalese temple and then from there to the image at which if one looked hard enough, one saw an 'Om' on the forehead. Then to another, which had artificial eyes but, which if one started at long enough, one was supposed to see the pupils move. Finally to an image from the pointed forefinger of which a drop of water would drip every forty–five minutes. Thence to the two sets of foot prints, one single and the other double belonging to Lord Vishnu and to Lord Buddha, both containing water, which it was said would not finish irrespective of how many devotees drank it. As they came to the Big Bell, said to have been placed there by demons, as humans would not be able to lift it, they both felt very tired. They were not the only ones, for there were other Burmese sitting out there and eating their rice out of little containers that resembled parts of tiffin carriers. Finally they went to the building which housed the various offerings made by the people. At long last, after this tour of this centre of the 'Phayas' or Gods, with its history of the 'Baluma' or Demons, they went to the fortune tellers in the precincts. From there the two went and offered flowers at the Shwe Sule Pagoda. The last in this series of Buddhists shrines was the World Peace Pagoda.

The next day was spent in going around the town – the Bandoola Park, Scott's and other markets. There was the usually motley crowd, always in a rush to get somewhere. This was more apparent in the evening for all the pavements were literally full of people. This was perhaps an exaggeration, for half the pavement was taken up by the pedlars selling their wares.

In the atmosphere prevalent at that time, it was a couple of days before they got passports endorsed to visit Nepal, India and Ceylon. Bir thought that the easiest route for the sake of his wife would be to take the steamer to Calcutta and then by train to the Indo-Nepal border.

Calcutta itself was a shock to Way Shin Yi. The scars of the 1947 partition of India were still visible in the form of refugees who happened to be everywhere. Was it just a question of overcrowding in a city offering limited facilities of housing and sewage disposal ? Bir had to offer to his wife Way Shin Yi a reasonable explanation as to why these people were sleeping and literally living on the streets, and the refugee reason seemed as good as any.

From Calcutta Bir and his wife took the 8 o'clock evening train going via Asansol to Patna. Reaching the station at nine the next morning they took two rickshaws and piling themselves and their goods into these, they proceeded towards Mahendru Ghat. The half hour over the dusty road, then the transfer into the steamer and a further one hour to cross the river Ganges and reach Pahlezaghat was quite an arduous journey at the relatively early hour of the morning. Then yet a third change into a train and another hour's trip to Sonepur. Again another change to get into the overnight one for Gorakhpur and finally another transfer into a train going to Nautanwa. The last leg of the journey was the crossing of the border into Nepal to a place called Bhairahawa. They then went by car through the first foot-hills of the Churiya hills to Lumbini, the birthplace of Gautam, the Buddha. Bir told his wife that it was in this wooded district of Sal trees that the Buddha was born in 623 B.C. The story went that Queen Maya Devi was going from her capital at Kapilvastu to her parents home, and while resting at Lumbini she gave birth to a child. There too was the massive stone pillar erected by the Indian Emperor Ashoka when he visited Lumbini in 249 B.C. By this time Ashoka had been converted into Buddhism for a good twenty years, and it was his zeal that that led to the propagation of the faith not only in India but spread far and wide to other countries in South and South-East Asia.

Then, of course, there was the temple of Maya Devi. There were devotees at this temple, laying flowers at the small stone relief showing the five main figures amongst which were Queen Maya Devi and the new born child. The bas relief was true to the traditional teaching that the delivery was in the upright position, for it showed Maya Devi supporting herself by holding on to a branch of a Sal tree. The newly born infant Buddha was also standing upright on a lotus pedestal against an oval halo, while other heavenly figures were shown pouring water and lotuses from vessels presumably from heaven.

From there they went to the newly built Buddhist temple. Besides it were the ruined walls, rectangular restored tank, and earth mounds, to see. After this rather quick tour Bir took Way Shin Yi to Tilaurakot. This is thought to be what was called in those days as Kapilavastu. This was the place where the young prince Siddhartha met the sick person; where Siddhartha competed with other youths of his age in sports and where the Buddha after his Enlightenment preached to his father. The remains of Kapilavastu offer adequate proofs of its having been a very active centre of Buddhist culture, with plenty of stupas and monasteries.

Two days at Lumbini were enough for them to see all they wanted. In fact, one day would have been enough, but because they had to obtain the airline ticket, they had to stay that extra half day. Bir Bahadur was happy to hear that his new-homeland Burma was helping in the development of Lumbini. He hoped that the day would come when all the major Buddhist nations of Asia and the many adherants to the faith elsewhere would help in making this a major place of pilgrimage for Buddhists. This would, Bir felt, help the fledgling tourist industry in Nepal. Visits to Lumbini, Kathmandu, Sarnath in Varanasi and then to Ceylon would be the main points in any Buddhist's itinerary. Bir was sure that he and his wife would not be able to make it to Ceylon this time, but perhaps at a later date he hoped to get there.

The flight from the dusty airfield at Bhairahawa to Bharatpur was a bare half hour. The flight in the Dakota plane brought back memories of the very same D.C. 3s and the war in Burma. A half hour halt in that hot airport terminal at Bharatpur and then the last leg of the journey to Kathmandu. As the plane entered the valley Bir pointed out Shimbhu and Boudha to his wife. Those massive stupas looked so small from the air, it seemed hardly possible that it was real buildings that they were looking at, and not just a model of the valley.

From the airport which had been renamed after the late King Tribhuvan, they took the airline transport to town and then registered at a small hotel in Juddha Road. During the course of that evening, Bir had during the course of half an hour's stroll, shown his wife all that there was to see of the shopping district of Kathmandu. Even to someone coming from Burma it all seemed so small and inadequate.

The next day Bir and his wife took a jeep on hire and went to the then so called Shimbhu, now Swayambhunath Stupa, on the small hillock to the west of Kathmandu. They had to go past what seemed like another parade ground, and it probably was judging by the fact that there were a few hutments there and a sort of gate in the middle of the ground. From the road that they were on, Bir could not make out which Battalion's emblem it was. He wondered then as to where the Kalibahadurs were. Then to the National museum, where they had a quick stroll. As they were leaving the compound Bir saw the huge bent girder, a relic of the 1934 earthquake. This brought to his mind the day on that hill when he and Chandra had seen the collapsing huts and he related the whole event to his wife. From there they could see the vast semi-circular structure of the stupa, surmounted by the gold gilt projection with the all seeing eyes of the Buddha looking into the four different directions. They stopped the jeep at the bottom of the hillock and then walked up the stone stairs past the two/three stone images of giants to the top. In the main quadrangle at the top there were a number of smaller stupas which had been added presumably by devotees over the years. Not only that but there were images of and temples to other Hindu gods. Bir reminded his wife that Buddha being considered a re-incarnation of Vishnu, it was but natural that all Nepalese whether they were basically Hindu or Buddhists paid homage here and elsewhere at other places in the country. This stupa was, according to legend, built at a spot where a lotus had bloomed when the whole valley of Kathmandu was a lake. Both Bir and his wife stood before a huge image in a side building and muttered 'Buddham Saranam Gacchami, Dhammam Saranam Gacchami, Sangham Saranam Gacchami' or 'I take refugee in the Buddha, I take refugee in His Law, I take refuge in his monk disciples'.

From there the two went to a place called Thainti. Here in one corner of a big quadrangle was a small stupa. They crossed this and went towards the entrance to Kathe Simbhu. There in the midst of a row of houses and in the gap were two columns on the top of which there were two metal lions holding flags or perhaps standards. From there Bir and his wife could see the stupa with two recesses in the front—one due east and the other slightly tilted towards the south-east. As they walked around the stupa they found three other recesses with images inside. In the courtyard there were a number of Chaityas, of various sizes and shapes and there were a number of people, all engaged in their daily prayer.

The next place of visit was to the Mahaboudha Stupa near to the Tundikhel. It was a bit of an anti-climax after the main stupa on the hill at Shimbhu, and infact rebuilt on the original site after the great earthquake which had completely razed it to the ground. The disturbing feature about this place of worship was that it seemed to have been taken over more or less by the grain-dealers of the valley of Kathmandu. There they were with their bagfuls of rice hanging from the two ends of a pole which they were carrying on their shoulders.

Leaving Kathmandu, the driver took them to the city of Patan. On the approach to the city, they saw the first of the four stupas said to have been built by the Indian Emperor Ashoka, after his conversion to Buddhism. This and the other three stupas at the four corners of Patan were visited in turn before they finally went to the Rudra Varma Mahavihar. There was in this place a courtyard with innumerable images of bronze and stone – a veritable gallery if ever there was one.

From there they went to the Hiranya Varna Mahavihar, This was at a place called Kwabahal. There was a golden image of the Lord Buddha and a big prayer wheel which was placed on a pedestal on the upper part of the vihar. What interested Way Shin Yi more was the intricate decorative patterns that were almost everywhere.

From Patan across the town and passing by the temple of Lord Pashupatinath, they went to the largest of the Buddhist chaityas in Nepal, perhaps in the world. It was resplendent in this the 2500 of the year of the celebration of the Birth, Enlightenment and Nirvana of the Buddha. The hemisphere here was different in the sense that in it were made about eighty? small recesses each bearing an image of the Buddha. Of course there were the prayer wheels around the whole structure which both Way Shin Yi and Bir turned as they went round muttering 'Om Mani Padma Hum'. This was the structure with its thirteen golden rings, and the umbrella at the very top which impressed Way Shin Yi most.

By the time that they returned to the hotel it had been a hectic day and both Bir and his wife Way Shin Yi were very tired and slept like logs. It was during their stay in Nepal that they read about a Gurkha soldier who had been found in the jungles of Burma. It so happened that the Government of Burma had been carrying out mopping up operations against the rebels. They had during the course of this come across a man living in a primitive hut in the midst of the jungle and wearing animals skins. They had tried to get him to talk but of no avail. They could not make out what his nationality or origin was, and so the only recourse was to hand-cuff him and take him back with them. He could after all have been Chinese, Japanese or even Nepali ? During the march back some of the men from talking in Burmese periodically lapsed into Nepali. It was during the first day's mealtime, when they were so talking that they noticed some facial expressions come over the man's face as someone uttered some words in Nepali, Then suddenly, without any warning whatsoever, this man jumped up and shouted, 'Ma pani Gorkhali' (I too am a Gorkhali). According to the papers the men of the patrol were overjoyed that they had, after all these years, found a man who was still in the jungle from the time of the World War II. He had then been repatriated back to the Gurkha Battalion that he had been a member of. This Gurkha Battalion was now a part of the Indian Army and the man concerned had been accepted back, then pensioned off, and finally sent back to Nepal.

Way Shin Yi and Bir having seen the places of pilgrimage at Kathmandu did not have much further interest in the city. The next place to go to was of course to Sarnath, near Varanasi in India. This stretch was no problem for they could take the Indian Airlines plane there. The trouble would be the distant train journey from there to Colombo. A pity that there was no direct flight from Kathmandu to Colombo, for that would have much simplified matters. Perhaps at some later date they would have to travel to Colombo.

The Fokkar Friendship plane to Varanasi did not take very long to get to the Bhagalpur Airport at Varanasi. Bir and Way Shin had intended to take the Airline transport back to the town, but the porter took them to a taxi and before they knew what, all their belongings and they themselves were in the taxi and speeding along the twelve mile route to the hotel. It was a drive across a countryside that was excessively dry, and the fact that they even saw camels carrying goods brought the fleeting thought to their heads that they were perhaps headed towards the desert. Cars seemed relatively few for such a big place as Varanasi—there seemed to be more human propelled bicycle rickshaws and horse drawn ekkas or tangas. The Crown Hotel that they were taken to was a remnant of the colonial days. The building itself was the standard type that the British had thought up for their colonial possessions such as India and Burma, and Bir and Way Shin Yi felt quite at home in it.

That first evening Bir took Way Shin Yi to see the Ghats. The multitude of people was in sharp contrast to the sparsely populated Burma that they were from. The crowds of worshippers rushing here and there to get their darshan, the peal of bells and finally the arrival at the holy Ganges was an experience in itself.

The queue of corpses at the ghats, waiting even after death, their turn to be turned to ashes was ironic in the sense that even after death one's difficulties in this world were not quite over. The pleasantest part of the evening was the boat ride from Pancha Ganga to Assi and back. As they got off the boat a man looked up at Bir and said 'Jaya Nepal'. Bir replied in response and soon they got talking. It transpired that the man was in charge of the Nepali Dharmasala at Dudhbinayak. On finding out that Bir was from Burma, Lamsalji, for that was the man's name invited Bir and Way Shin Yi to the dharmasala for a cup of tea.

They walked the few steps from the ghat and then through some winding alleys to the Dharmasala itself. This was a small building complex and as they reached it Bir realised that it was full of visitors—all Nepalese to a man and woman.

As they sat in Lamsalji's office and got talking, Bir realised that this genial nondescript individual was in fact a character in himself. He had travelled far and wide, not only in Nepal but also in parts of India and Burma, wherever there were Nepalese.

Being highly impressed Bir complimented him and ended off by saying' "You certainly have done a lot for the Nepalese community out here."

"I suppose so, if you look at it that way. But it has been an uphill task most of the time. I remember the initial days. How the idea came into my head I don't know, but I had a Brownie camera, one of the very first ones to come out. I went all over the place, taking photographs of all the Nepalese and asking them for contributions to build this place. They were generous and I in turn have placed their snaps on the walls. See that one out there. That's one of Juddha Shumsher—he gave me quite a sum. There in the corner are some of the Nepalese people in Burma, who gave me funds also.

"Well to come back to the story, I got the funds and then

got the building up. Things were going quite well, and then some persons of the business community got interested in this Dharmasala, for they could then utilise the funds. I was booted out and then it was a question of making hay whilst the sun shines. This group had not liked the fact that whilst I was doing this work I was to a certain extent supporting my family. I begged and collected money but I built this whole complex and deposited some appreciable funds. This new group, of so .called volunteers did not take any pay but they frittered away the funds in dinner parties, meetings and other functions almost all the money that this trust had. It was an odd group with odd ideas. Some people realised this and one particular businessman, whom I shall not name then spent enough money to enrol new members to such an extent that particular group was voted out the next time. Now the constitution has been revised and such articles incorporatəd that it is almost impossible for such an eventuality to recur in future."

Bir and Way Shin Yi listened to the story and then giving some donation to this dharmasala, made their way back to the hotel. Lamsalji in his turn made them promise that if they came to Varanasi again, they would write and inform him beforehand, so that he would reserve a room for them. As they returned to the hotel, both husband and wife thought that it had been a full, pleasant and varied day.

The next day they set out once again by taxi for Sarnath. The first stop was at a place called Sita Rasoi where there was a big arch which one could climb. Then the visit to the museum there and thence to Khandahar. The Jain temple was near by and following this they came to the stupa which Emperor Ashoka had put up. Then came the Vihar to Lord Buddha followed by another made to him. They came finally to the temple to Sarang Nath or Shivaji. This outing had also been hectic and had taken the whole afternoon.

On the morrow they took to Gaya a taxi for the explicit purpose of seeing the site of the sacred 'Buddhi' tree. It was a drive to and fro along dusty roads cutting through the parched and dry countryside. The very next day Bir and his wife took the four o'clock Doon Express which hurtled through the countryside and brought them via Mogulsarai, Gaya, Dhanawat, Asansol and then to Howrah, Calcutta. The return trip by steamer was uneventful and Bir and Way Shin Yi soon found themselves back in Burma.

8

Life for the ordinary ethnic Nepali was not bad in Burma. They were getting a fair deal for most of them, being farmers and small fry, were able to eke out a reasonable living from the land, and maintain a certain standard. They had retained their own customs, and it was a fact which the Burmese accepted. Marriage to a Burmese girl, however, as in the case of Bir, and a handful of others, was quite rare. When any such marriage took place, the other members of each community took it upon themselves to ponder over the motives. Then there was of course the Burmisation of what had been a Nepali name. The question was whether it was the action of a community in a quandary. Could it be equated with the action of the Anglo-Burmans and their attempts to pass themselves off as English, during all the years that the overseas masters were there? On the other hand, the changing of names was not very unusal in a Buddhist society. After all, every one, irrespective of his nationality, took a Buddhist name once he accepted the faith and became a monk of the order. All said and done, however. the Burmese looked with a kindly eye and attitude towards the Nepalese, for Nepal was after all the place their God, Lord Buddha was born.

The first ripple in this area of tranquility rose when the Calcutta Matric and the Senior Cambridge examinations were abolished, and Burmese became a compulsory subject at school. The Nepalese community accepted this, for they were, after all, in Burma and had to keep to the customs and laws of the land. Then came the nationalisation of schools and finally to cap it all came the re-organisation of the 4th Gurkha Regiment and the installation of Burmese officers. This was the final straw. For the others, like the Indians, the banning of trade by foreigners, and the nationalisation of their houses and shops on the 2nd of March 1962, was the hardest blow. The 5000 Kyat compensation wss mearge, but the most ironic part was for them to be made managers of what had once been their own businesses or shops.

Bir Bahadur was affected by the 1962 changes in the sense that to continue working at Mogok and carry on his ruby business, he had to opt for Burmese citizenship. This was no problem for after all his wife was Burmese by birth. Bir felt that there would be much more in the way of stringent checks in the future, so that it would not henceforth be so easy to divert gems from the regular sources to underhand dealings. It was then that his wife and he decided to shift their house, and go to live at Tambhu.

The demonetisation of currency notes in April, 1962 was meant to affect mainly the Indian and Chinese hoarders of Burma. They were the people who controlled business—the real economic masters of the market and, as such, were not very popular. They were thepeople who held on to the stacks of 100 and even 50 Kyats notes. All such notes had to be exchanged for lower denomination ones, and to this was added the stipulation that only 500 Kyats would be given back in exchange per person, irrespective of how much was handed in. For 100 and 50 Kyats denomination notes in large numbers, one had to provide reasons for possessing them, or otherwise many questions would be asked. Many therefore burned or threw the paper money away into the river, or gave them away to certain Nepalese or Indians at a certain percentage, at the then existing rate of 600 Kyats for Rs. 100.

One way was to give it to a trader who had an account in India. This man would then give a letter with some code word, and when the person concerned went to India he got the money. The trader involved would get 60,000 Kyats for 10,000 Rupees I.C. With this money the local trader would buy the best of the sapphires or rubies - perhaps even the rare blood red or crimson ruby and smuggle it across the border at Assam, or sell it there at a profit. Some, it was rumoured, sent these jewels in diplomatic pouches.

Bir Bahadur felt that there was some quick and easy money to be made out of this. One of the snags was that because Bir Bahadur had opted for Burmese citizenship, there was no question of him going by the normal route for the simple reason that he would not be able to get a passport. He would have to blaze his own trail. He decide to test the route and felt that a convenient point would be at a place which was right there - at Tambhu on the Burmese border. He was not carrying anything this time, for his intention was not to be caught with anything on him. At Tambhu, Bir met a Nepali lad who was also returning and who had about Rs. 20,000 in precious stones. He heard from the lad that most of the people leaving Burma usually sent their family members by plane and brought most of their worldly goods such as gold, diamonds and other precious stones via the land route at Tambhu. For example a lot of the Burma returned Nepalese had set themselves up at Kathmandu, Bhairahawa, Hetauda, and others at Biratnagar, and seemed to be living in great style, in great opulence, for they owned houses, cars, trucks, buses etc. They could get some nasty shocks if any one delved and found out their roots, and how they had collected all this material wealth. This was of least concern to Bir, for he himself was about to embark on such an undertaking himself. He would not restrict himself to the Nepalese wanting to return to Nepal, but would rather work for the Marwari traders for that was where the money was. Bir felt that the journey from Burma must be made through Tambhu, and through the Naga area for with all the turmoil going on, he would be able to slip through all the confusion. Perhaps he might even be able to make contact with the Nagas.

Tambhu, some 635 miles from Mandalay, was itself small and most of the people, generally Burmese army pensioners of Nepalese descent, tended to keep shops there, or were involved in agriculture. The rice-stubble on the recently mowed fields bore evidence of this. Besides rice and the other main crop was of course wheat. This was just frontage, for the actual work was to bring stuff from Burma and take it to various places in India or Nepal at the hefty commission of 20–30%. This stuff could vary from whole heads of cattle, spare parts for engines, or even whole diesel engines, and, of course, gems.

Bir decided that if he involved himself in this work, which he was almost sure he would, then he and his wife Way Shin Yi would shift from Maymyo and come out here. Bir also obtained an Indian Identity Card from one of the Nepalese and made himself (once again) into a certain bookseller named Deepak from Darjeeling. He also bought a pair of jeans, a fancy polyester T shirt, a denim jacket and a peaked golf cap with the words 'Saigon Country Club' pasted on it. Bir was quite confident that he would get through, for to travel with such an identity card was nothing unusual. A lot of labourers on both the Indian and Burmese side of the border did it; for all one had to do was to produce one's identity card and one could go across for twelve hours at a stretch. Bir had not yet made any arrangement with the four forces of the Burmese border viz. the customs, the security guards, the military and the police, for he felt he could leave this for the next time when he would be carrying something. Bir crossed the small Tambhu river on foot for there was no bridge and went on to the Indian side at Premnagar and thence to Moreh. In a matter of twenty minutes he was there.

The bus was due to leave the next morning at 7.00. Bir got to the bus stop and took his place well ahead of time. He was therefore somewhat taken aback when a couple of C.I.D. fellows came and took him off the bus and together with his goods carted him off to the local police station. After being first surrounded Bir was then stripped naked by four armywallahs. He did not say anything, but wondered if he had been mistaken for someone else, perhaps for the lad with Rs. 20,000 in precious stones. Even when the questionings started, Bir was stilled puzzled. The words were certainly harsh and unfriendly.

A man, presumably the CID inspector asked, "Who are you and why have you come here?"

Bir, having now to play up to his Indian Identity Card said, "My name is Deepak and I come from Darjeeling. I have a book store there. I came here to see what the market was for Indian and Nepali books. I also do some printing in Darjeeling."

"You bastard, you are not an ordinary bookseller. You are an imposter, a CID from another country."

Bir, did not reply immediately. He did not know anything about the person Deepak, whose identity he had taken. Perhaps that particular man had come here and created trouble. Perhaps he had also other accomplices. Bir felt like a blind man grooping about and, at least to keep up this pretence, he said, "I am not a CID. I am an ordinary bookseller. My identity card says that."

The ill-tempered officer came forward and tried to give a couple of slaps to Bir. Bir managed to duck, and thus was not on the receiving end. The officer, more annoyed than ever, came forward threateningly.

The other officer, presumably a subordinate, who was looking on now said, "No Sir, he is a foreigner. He is really a Nepali with forged Indian papers."

Hearing this, the slapping happy officer of Nepalese descent too, mumbled, "Sorry" and went away.

By this time Bir had already missed the bus. He was however still surrounded, for they still thought Bir to be a CID. The fact that he was wearing the cap with the words SAIGON still heightened their suspicions. They thought that he was a CID from Saigon. Bir with a wry smile on his lips took this to be a compliment, if he was taken for 'Our Man in Saigon'.

The little money that remained with him, his identity card, and the bus ticket were, however, taken away. It was only after that, that the surrounding guards were taken off. The two officers got busy and wrote or noted something for almots two hours. Bir's feet were aching, but who was he to complain? As his eyes wandered here and there, he saw the jeep outside and noted that the keys were in the ignition. Bir's brain toyed wtth the idea of killing these two nincompoops and escaping in the jeep, for he felt it would only be a question of time before they killed him. Would his trying to escape give them the reason that they were looking for, the reason to pull the trigger on him? One of the reasons that Bir banished this thought from his mind was because he really did not know how much fuel there was in the tank of the jeep.

The hours of waiting seemed to be over when he was at last taken away from there at just about noon. But it was a case of from the frying pan into the fire, for he was carried by a guard to the nearby police station, and locked in a cubicle which was barely three feet by three feet. Even when he was inside, they queried about that forged pass and wanted to know where the other two persons named, a certain Rupa and Billa were. Not knowing anything about them, let alone their whereabouts, Bir said that he had just met them whilst coming from Dimapur to cross the Naga region, and after finding that they were all coming to the same place, had made the pass and trip together.

In the cubicle next to Bir's there was a Manipuri Naga called Meku who had come to Moreh without permission. He was a businessman and had relatives at Moreh. He introduced Bir to his sister Niking when she came to visit him. Their father was a Naga, but their mother, who was now dead, had been a Nepali. As a result Meku had had some contact with the Nepalese, most of whom came there to do work either as labourers or as woodsmen to Naga contractors. This immediately created an invisible bond of affinity between Meku, Niking and Bir. Niking who looked a kindly girl smiled at Bir—a gesture which made her the more beautiful, though rather primitive in her ornamental necklace of conch shells and corals.

That same evening Meku gave Rs. 100 to the jail officer and fled from there. Before fleeing, however, he informed Bir that he had instructed Niking to look after, and help him if required. It was no surprise to Bir therefore, when at about nine that evening Niking brought him some bread, a double omelette and coffee. Whilst Bir ate, she cried a little and said how sorry she was that he was in such a predicament. Bir then toyed with the idea of fleeing from the jail too; but then felt that this was a hopeless proposition, for he could be easily killed by the Nagas. Restless thoughts kept him awake most of the night, although the very stillness all around was rather eerie A strange atmosphere indeed with no howling stray dogs around. Bir vaguely recalled having been told that the Nagas kept their dogs in and locked, as they were a good source of meat.

The next morning Niking was there with breakfast. Bir was pleasantly surprised for he had not been looking forward to the prison fare of the 6 o'clock tea and one slice of bread; and the nine and three o'clock menus of rice, dal and vegetables. Bir was truly thankful to Niking. After having eaten, he talked to the jail officer and subsequently to the CIDs and convinced them that he was a Nepali and so was set loose on his own surety. Once he was free, Niking, in true keeping to she wishes of her brother Meku, took him to the small hotel that she ran, and gave him a good, square meal. They got talking on friendly terms, and Niking offered Rs. 50,000 if Bir could take her to Nepal, show her around the various places there and then bring her back to Calcutta. From there she would make her own back. It was a good proposal but Bir had no hope of getting out from there alive, let alone take someone along with him. On second thoughts, however, Bir felt that if he fled from there with her, then Niking would be his protection during any possible encounter with the Nagas. From what Bir had seen of them, he was virtually sure that he would need it. They seemed primitive enough, going round virtually naked most of the time. The men used to tie a string around the waist with possibly a piece of torn cloth, judging by the fact that the two ends of it were hanging both in front and at the back over the private parts. The women, though primitive had one advantage of seemingly being aware of the latest fashion, viz. they were all sporting a short skirt and going topless. Then there was the cross-bow that the men carried. Bir was frightened, for he had heard that the tips of the arrows had a very fast acting and effective poison smeared on to it. Last but not least was the fact these Nagas were head-hunters. After all, Bir had heard hair raising stories of the Sawlaw tribes of the Burmese Nagas, who had come into India on head-hunting forays.

Bir soon discarded the idea of taking Niking with him for he felt sure that such action on his part would put her in bad with the Indian authorities. Bir had truly come to like the girl, theirs was a platonic or a brother/sister type relationship, and he could not bear the thought of any harm befalling her. Niking told him a lot about their ways and customs, why the Nagas liked community singing, dancing and of course the rice wine. Bir even took food on the traditional plates with their short wooden legs and with wooden spoons. The meat preparation was very nice but he did not ask what it was, for fear that it may have been cow's, dog's or even rat's meat. All said and done, he spent most of the day with her at the hotel; for her father used to go out most of the time to look after his business.

The third day however the police came and said that they were taking him to Imphal. Niking could not control her tears, and came to the bus stop to see him off in the company of the officers of the law. Bir promised that he would be back to see her, and then climbed into the bus. As the bus moved off and gained momentum, he could see Niking, a lonely figure with her head turned down and crying. As the bus turned round a band, Bir saw her lift her right hand to her eyes, as thought wiping away the tears and then turn slowly round and go back homewards. Even Bir, a very unemotional man felt sad and forlorn. He had no tears but Niking would always come to occupy a place in his heart. Niking was a simple, innocent person with nothing but the essential goodness of her heart, and one who had never come face to face with hard cruel world.

As the bus moved on it soon started to drizzle. Bir was in his own mind praying to God, that the Almighty in his kindness would get the Naga rebels to attack the bus. Trying to make the best of an uncomfortable situation, Bir asked the policemen about his possible fate.

One of the officers with a grin on his face replied, "The worst, I suppose, is that you could be shot in an attempt of trying to escape. More likely, however, is that you will get about six years of imprisonment. You can console yourself with the thought that the situation would not have been any different had you been caught by the Burmese. These forged papers would have meant that you would have disappeared without a trace and the driver of the bus on which you were travelling would have suffered a lot of hardship and ill treatment from the authorities, although it was of course none of his fault."

Bir did not bother to start up a conversatian after this, As soon as they reached Imphal at about four in the afternoon, Bir was taken straightaway to the court there. There was the same repetition of questions, almost word for word. After a while Bir got fed up and said that if they did not shut up he would either try to commit suicide or go on a hunger strike. The judge who seemed to be a kindly man admonished him with a warning that he could be held for contempt of court. Then after a discussion the judge said that only after the others named in the pass had been rounded up, would Bir be set free. Bir, wanted to shout out that this was impossible, but because of the previous warning decided that he would hold his tongue and let events take their course. On second thoughts, the judge told the guard to take Bir to an adjoining room where he asked Bir if he knew anyone who would stand surety for him. In such an eventuality the judge said that Bir could be set free on bail for a period of seven days. When Bir said that he had no one, the judge left him there and went out. Bir then tried to tempt his guard by showing some money and tried to talk him into standing surety for him. It was no dice.

After a couple of minutes, four other men, presumably CIDs, came and talked in the Naga tongue. One of them turned round to Bir and said that they would let him stay out for a few days, but that he must make no attempt whatsoever to leave town. Bir agreed, but he was sure that this sudden change of heart must be because they were expecting him to lead to the people named in that acursed pass. What had he, Bir, to lose anyway ? On getting Bir's consent the man went to the judge and said that matters had been sorted out, but that Bir would first have to go to the police station to have some photographs taken. Bir was quite game to that.

When they reached the police station there was a man with a camera, waiting there for them. It seemed an expensive and up-to-date gadget and Bir asked to have a look at it, feigning at being a great photographic 'bug'. The cameraman, who felt rather important at having such equipment, handed it to Bir to have a look. Bir asked a few questions looked the camera over, left the speed setting as it was, but surreptitiously changed the lens opening to large at F 1.4 before giving it back to the cameraman. Bir, was a little unneasy for if the man was a real professional he might decide to re-check the settings, and thus find out the change even before taking the first shot. The popping of flash-lights denoted not one but two shots taken from different angles, Bir was convinced that the man was definitely an amateur. Bir was convinced too that his snaps were spoilt but the big question was when they would find out. He was sure that the man had just put in a 36 exposure film into the camera, and unless they took shots of a lot of so called miscreants like him, it was unlikely that the roll would be finished soon. Bir was laughing to himself for this was certainly a bit of quick thinking on his part.

Bir was then set loose but these four idiots of CIDs were always there in turns of twos to tail him. At the dharmasala even, two would be inside their room which was next door to his, whilst the other two would be roaming around the compound. Bir went to the cinema and they came to sit in some rows at the back. Bir went to eat and they took a table in full sight of him. Even when he went to the loo (toilet), Bir presumed that they were waiting outside, for they were always there when he came out of the door. Bir deduced that their expectation was that he would either try to commit suicide, or try to head for the Indian Airlines office or the bus station. Bir suspected that the CIDs had explicit instructions to take him into custody the moment he went so much as near to those places.

Bir thought of various ways to try to escape but the constant checking of the CIDs made him think twice before even bringing such ideas into his head. From time to time, one of them, who presumably was acting as a spokesman, even suggested that they might look the other way in return for Bir's Rolex Seamaster watch plus some ready cash. Bir was however bidding his time and preparing the ground for an attempt at escape.

During the course of his roamings in the town Bir had noted that there was a new English film at a cinema hall which was conveniently near to the bus station. It was on the sixth day of his circumscribed freedom that Bir went to see that particular film. Sure enough the CIDs came in also but once the film had started, Bir on some pretext changed places with the man who was sitting next to him. After a decent interval Bir quietly went out of the hall, and walked quickly to the office of the bus depot that was just outside. At the bus stop two army personnel were buying tickets and they were Gurkhas, he was sure. He got talking, and after giving them the money requested if they would be kind enough to buy his ticket as he was in a frightful hurry. They agreed and as their army line was small, Bir got his ticket in no time at all. Hearing that they too were going to Dimapur,

Bir made out that he just had to rush, but could they meet him in room no. 3 of of the dharmasala. Hearing such a request Bir noticed that they were momentarily taken aback but he did not wait to explain further.

Bir rushed back to the hall and it appeared that the two CIDs, entrusted to tail him were oblivious of his absence. After the film, Bir went back to his room and waited, hoping against hope that the two army men he had met at the bus station would heed his request and come. The evening dragged on, and, at last, when they finally did come, his elation knew no bounds. Bir told them all that he had had to go through, and asked for their help in just getting back to Nepal. They did not give any reply, either yes or no. After some time they opened the small suitcases that they were carrying, and started arranging the uniforms that were inside. Seeing this an idea was forming in Bir's mind. For its success it was essential that the lads should stay there overnight, so Bir in true generous fashion suggested that they could stay there. Now that it was dark, Bir then sneaked out of tne dharmasala and had a proper hair cut—a regular short back and sides. When he returned, without his long hair, Bir looked a much younger and different person.

Bir then talked with one of the army men to loan him his dress and aid him Bir, in getting out. The whole plan was outlined and discussed. The next day when they came out of the dharmasala, Bir was dressed as a personnel of the Border Security Force, complete with the badge on his cap and shoulders. The tinted glasses which he was wearing also helped to hide his true identity. Bir carried the army man's stuff and vise versa. The CIDs had no inkling whatsoever that they had been given the slip. It was plain going to the bus stop, and the bus too started punctually at 6.00 a. m. After about two hours on the road, a jeep came up and asked them to stop. Because Bir was with the army man and in an uniform, he was given but a cursory glance as was also the genuine army man at his side. Some totally innocent man, or perhaps some one involved in something else totally different, was taken off that bus on suspicion and carted off to their police jeep. This was one of the routes to get out of Manipur and there were three other checks. Bir made up his mind that the next time he would use some other route.

At the Manipur railway station there were some policemen with rather blurred photographs in their hands. Bir saw one from quite a distance and wondered if it was his. Bir and his companion in the army dress had full right to an empty army compartment but saying that the other man was with them they somehow managed to get him in. Once the train started, Bir changed back into civilian clothes and returned the army dress to the army man, who promptly put it on. As soon as Silguri was reached, Bir, after thanking his friends got hurriedly out of the train and out of the station. He then got on a taxi and made his way to Karkar Vitha. After spending a few days there Bir decided that it was now time to go back, and try anothnr route, or perhaps distribute a bit of money to people all along the line, so that there would be no one really interested in stopping him. After all it is but natural not to cut the hand that feeds one.

9

Having done the Tambhu to Nepal trip and undaunted in spite of the hardships he had on this intial journey, Bir's mind was made up. With the shift to Tambhu, Bir started off in this new venture. There were quite a few people with Foreigners Registration Certificates (F. R. C.) who were wanting to get out of Burma. They could get passports but were only allowed to take out about twelve and a half pounds of gold per individual. This was a generous allowance to anyone of moderate means but the crux of the problem were the people who had had plenty tucked away. It was rumoured that quite a bit of the stuff, both money and jewels, went through official channels, but whether it was or could be collected at the other end was a different matter. Rather than do business on such risky deals, quite a few of the persons were willing to deal with the middle men. These people, like Bir Bahadur, were willing to take gems and what not across the border and to places as far apart as Kathmandu, Chandigarh or Bombay. Bir's cut out of this was of course the usual 25·/. taken by everyone in this line. As time went on Bir became better known and completely trusted by his many contacts amongst the Marwari community at Bombay, Calcutta and Kathmandu.

But Bir Bahadur was getting richer at the cost of a certain pride. True, the mode of his and his wive's lives had changed in that they were much more comfortably off. They were both aware of the tremendous risks that they had been taking. At times they felt that the secret police were behind them but on second thoughts had confidence in themselves, and felt that it was just undue cautiousness on their part. Both Bir Bahadur and his wife Way Shin Yi had their National Registration Certificates (N. R. C.) and their numbers. It was therefore a matter of just twenty-four to seventy-two hours before the police would be knocking on their doors or laying their hands on them, had they come across any irregularities or had they wanted to.

Whenever Bir Bahadur and a few of his cronies met at a club of some sort, they always referred to themselves by their Nepali names. Bir's identity card listed him as Maung Tin Win. There two views on this and though a friend of Bir called Lal (Red) Bahadur Limbu was Maung Myint Thein, it was pleasant to hear the pros and cons of this argument.

"I feel sometimes that though the government is out after the traders it is also partly acting against us. This is unfair for we have after all being trying to fit in with the Burmese mainstream of life," said Bir by way of throwing the gauntlet.

Lal took it up immediately. 'I don't agree with you. I think that what the government is doing is correct. After all we did opt for Burmese citizenship. We thought that we would get benefits if we did so. There is unfortunately a deep-seated feeling against Indian traders. The initial fault was that of the Indian money-lenders or Chettairs who gained control of a lot of the rice lands of the Irrawaddy delta during the depression of 1929. Now the method is more subtle. The Burmese frontman gets the licence and sells it to his Indian counterpart, who subsequently remits the foreign exchange to his exporter abroad. The money goes out but what is sent, just to complete the formalities are crates containing a lot of rubbish such as waste paper and rags. Of course most of the people involved must see eye to eye with one another, for any such scheme to succeed. How would you feel if this was Nepal and they had control of all the business. It is, as you know, all Import and Export, employing only just two or three people. The money is just restricted to the betterment of this money squeezing elite. What should be done is that they should be made to involve themselves in the establishment of industries. Only then will the country be better off in the form of jobs for its people and real national benefit."

"Come Lal, it is not as simple as that. I think that the action was against the Indians, the ones who were Hindus, rather than the Burmese and the Muslims. It was more a sort of pent up feeling against people who practised discrimination of a sort–the discrimination of untouchability. Take the case of an Indian Hindu living with a Burmese girl. He sleeps with her, but does not eat the food prepared by her nor drink water touched by her. Is that not hypocrisy ? Don't you think that we Nepalese deserved a better deal. After all we were fighting for them, with them, for saving Burma from the grasp of the Japanese. Is this what we deserve for thanks ?"

"Why do we people of Gorkhali stock always harp back on this? We seem to have a chip on our shoulder about all this. They have not treated us that badly. They know that we Gurkhas are not so rigid in our views nor so intolerant in our upbringing. After all most of us of Nepalese origin were different, for we were living in villages and were in the army and the police—hence we have not been made to feel the brunt. We have also been regarded as a reliable, hardworking lot. We of Nepalese stock were just seeking a living and not living on the fat of the land. You all know me well, but let us for a moment think of my story.

"It was in 1936. I had come to Kathmandu with another village lad and whilst there we met someone who asked us if we would be prepared to go to Birgunj and thence to Calcutta. Seeing that this had been our original intention when we set out from the village, the man did not have to coax us and so we soon found ourselves in Calcutta. At that time there was no question of passports, no registration certificates and after a few days there we met another Nepali who gave us money for fares, an address in Rangoon and told us to go there. We paid the Rs. 16 fare and hopped on the steamer to Rangoon. Three days of the high seas, and we reached the place— Rangoon, the 'Last of the War.' How ironic, but the War of Wars, a war in which Burma was to be directly involved, had not yet started. I still remember it as if it were yesterday. When we had been on the river a little while our first view was of the Syriam pagoda on the east, then, far ahead to the north on a knoll overlooking the town, was the glittering, golden Shwedagon. After weaving our way through the hive of activity at this portion, past the rice mills, the great municipal bazaar, the banks, the post and telegraph officers, the courts,— various other government offices, including the customs, we finally reached the quay where the steamer docked.

"As we stepped ashore we saw a few army recruiters wanting to get us for the army. To try to get us to enlist, they literally chased us around during the course of the three days that we were there. The existence of the Gurkhas barracks on the Prome Road was proof enough that we were wanted in Burma. Realising that the man whose address we had, probably had similar intentions, we decide to go further into the unknown and towards Maymyo. We took the old steam engine drawn train, with its many haltages and after nearly twenty-four hours reached our destination.

"It was something for which we were totally unprepared, –a small Nepal in the midst of Burma. There was Nalabasti, Jhilbasti and Barbhatta. There were a lot of people from Nepal out there and it was easy in those days to settle down in Burma. One went to the edge of the jungle, cleared a plot of land grew what one could during the two to three years that one was there. Once the quality of the soil decreased because the nutrients had been taken out by the repeated plantings, leading thus to lower and lower yields, the Nepalese community on the periphery moved further outwards into virgin land. My friend and I were tempted to settle down especially as we saw that the people of Nepalese origin had maintained their traditions. Dasain was celebrated more enthusiastically then even in Nepal. It was a communtty affair. A number of families say twenty or thirty clubbed together, kept the jamara at a specific place and also did pooja to Goddess Durga there. Then on the day of Phulpati, the persons went in a procession as far away as eight miles to get the phulpati. It was a wondrous sight. a whole group of people making merry and dancing to the accompaniment of music played by those who were in the army or police band and who had come home for the festival, bringing the phulpati back. Then on the day of the Tika everyone collected at the place where the jamara was kept and it was all done there.

"Dasain was followed soon after by the Burmese Diwali. It was called the festival of lights and celebrated in style. The Diwali of the Nepalese community or Bhai Tika was no less an important affair, and even in those days 'Bhailo Magne' for three continuous days was something akin to the carol singing of the Christians. The people would go from house, singing and collecting money for some cause. We celebrated the Nepalese New Year to and probably more heartily perhaps than even in Nepal. The reason for this was because our New Year fell during the time of the Burmese Thingyan Water Festival. It was therefore a time of general revelry – they celebrated in their style and we celebrated in our way. Our traditions, our customs are something which we have maintained over the years even upto now. We, of Nepalese origin, have always maintained our little niche out here. I don't think that we have a right to ask for any quarter.".

Moti Bahadur, also known as Soe Tin Htay, now entered the fray. "I think, Bir, that what Lal says is correct. It is perhaps because you don't have any children that you have not realised the full implications of the situation. Think of your child going to school, and using his usual Nepali name. He or she would never be accepted as a full–blooded Burmese, which we all technically are, Furthermore, those of our children who have tried to adjust themselves meet against some inborn, unexpected resistance from us. If they did intermarry they find themselves between two communities, the members of which create a sort of invisible wall in between. Things are worse for any children of such a marriage. Being neither wholly Nepalese nor wholly Burmese, they find themselves in a quandary. They have fallen between two stools or as we Nepalese say, they are neither a duck or a chicken. We only have to take a look at ourselves. We still refer to each other by our old names. Is it because we are too old to change or is it because we form a pocket of resistance in this land which is Burma ? My feeling is that things might get worse later. The old generation knew what we did for Burma and treats us accordingly. The ones born after the war have no inkling of this. It would not surprise me if one fine day we too are asked to pack up and go."

It was Bir's turn to give vent to his feelings. "Yes, but is it not a bit too much ? After all when I visited Nepal in 1956 and when I went to the various Buddhist shrines with my wife, they accepted her with open arms. True, her name was Way Shin Yi on the passport but the fact that she could speak Nepali meant that to them she was Nepali. This is, I think, a good trait and creates a feeiing of brotherhood with all the Nepalese in India and the rest of South East Asia. Not only that, any foreigner speaking Nepali is taken on equal terms. The question of being able to write the language does not seem to matter."

"Well, that still does not go against this argument. I think that if there are Nepalese citizens with foreign sounding names, they should on their own accord change it to something which is more Nepali sounding. Other people also change names for example on joining religious orders and becoming medicants of the Buddhist, Hindu or Anand Margi sects. Others simplify it, for example in place such as U.K. or U.S.A. they anglicise names such as 'Battenburg' and make it Mountbatten. We in Nepal also have our nwaran or horoscope name and our day-to-day or calling names. The Burmese too, change their names from time to time. The nadu or horoscope name is one which they use till about Puberty and then they change it. Sometimes this change, as you know, takes place much later, as in the case of Maung Sawka who became Maung Byaung," replied Lal Bahadur.

"Or perhaps everyone should have a common Nepali name. This could be name like Bir or Bahadur," rejoined Moti Bahadur.

"I should be happy with such a suggestion, seeing that everyone would then be named after me. Neverthelese I would not agree, for the generic name for any Nepalese in India was Bahadur and it is only now-a-days that, perhaps for the sake of variety, they have started calling some Kanchas. And then, lets face it: What is a Nepalese name ? I think that basically the Nepalese are a very tolerant and adaptable race. We have Hindus, Buddhists, Muslims and even Christians. A name like Peter or Ali would be just as Nepalese as Belaiti Man, Soviet Man, Verona, Tito Bahadur or even Hitler Man."

A few days later Bir went off to Bombay on another jaunt, carrying gems—rubies, jade and pokhraj or white stone. The person with whom he was staying at Bombay got a coded telegram saying that the Marbari counter-part had been jailed and a warrant was out for him, Bir Bahadur, too. A second telegram came stating that the Marbari involved had been shot.

Bir Bahadur did not dare to go back to Burma and his Burmese wife Way Shin Yi. He went instead to Kathmandu carrying the quite considerable amount of cash which was his commission. Reaching Kathmandu, his first action was to open a Bank Account and deposit most of the money that he was carrying with himself. He then went to the ex-serviceman's hostel which he knew was at Thamel, but he made out that he had been in the old Indian Brigade of Gurkhas and had spent some time in Burma. Bir got friendly with a certain Chet Bahadur who had been in India in the Gurkha Regiments also. This

Chet was an extrovert individual, and was, because of his short stature also referred to as Pudke. It was from Chet that Bir heard that cock fighting was also prevalent in Kathmandu. There was apparently in that same Tole of Kathmandu, a local leutenant colonel who was very fond of this from of sport. Hearing that such fights were generally held on a Saturday morning, Bir talked Chet into taking him there the coming Saturday. Bir had decided that he too would acquire a male cock and give it drugs to make it fight. He could give it some anabolics to make it look double its size too.

When Bir and Chet arrived promptly at 7.00 a.m. on the next Saturday morning. they saw a handful of people there. There were one or two people with cockrels under their crooked arms, but it was a chyakhura fight that was taking place. The chyakhura, a variety of partridge fight did not appear to be interesting most of the time for one bird was after the other—just trying to obstruct its passage to wherever it wanted to go. The birds would take short quick steps, both with their heads and necks tilted to one side and then push to obstruct each other. Occasionally one would manage to hold the head of the other with its beak and thus bring things to a standstill. In a fit of excitement, one would suddenly give a few kicks to the other. The spectators were for the most part silent and watched the proceedings sitting on their haunches on the ground. After some time one chyakhura, feeling, it had enough, rushed forward, followed close behind by the other. Then the second one would catch hold of it and the whole thing would start again. At other times, the one which felt that it had enough would then rush and take refuge in between the knees of one of the spectators, sitting on his haunches. Finally one of the birds decided that it had enough and would call it a day. It rushed headlong and weaving its way out of the ring of spectators it hid in a clump of bushes. The fight was over, the vanquished chyakhura was caught once again and put back in its cage. It would in all likelihood be exchanged for a young or a new one that someone had brought all the way from Jumla. After all a lot of the Nepalese still believed that if there was a chyakhura in the house, it would keep away illness from the children of the family. Besides that another more compelling reason was that lightning would not strike a house in which there was a chyakhura. For the average poor Nepali, it was a better and cheaper way to invest in a chyakhura than in lightning conductor.

The cock fights were much better. There were not the regular local cockrels but rather ones that had been bought from Lucknow in India or even further afield as Bangkok. They were not the minature bantam Thai cocks but rather the big ones, showing their flesh covered breast bone. Bir remembered too that the cocks they used to get fighting in Burma were like these. And regular bets they used to have on them in Burma. Funny how he remembered all this so vividly. A section of the Nepalese community had maintained cock fighting or ram fighting there. Bir wondered about ram fighting. It was something which had been in vogue Nepal at the time of Bhimsen Thapa and though not very popular now in Kathmandu, it still existed in parts of Burma. Bir pondered too about what happened here whether it was all above board or if there was any trickery which he as a newcomer would never be able to find out. The only way he could do so would be by joining them by buying a game cock himself. If you can't beat them join them.

No sooner thought of, than the solution presented itself. Chet had spent some time in India, so the logical course was to get Chet to go there and get a bird from there. The promise of a free trip to near Lucknow, some extra spending money at the rest houses of Hazratgunj, was enough to entice Chet. Of course the game cocks would have to be obtained from the surrounding villages, but Chet was fully capable of doing that.

It was not long before Chet Bahadur was back with not one, but two splendid specimens of game cocks. The following morning Bir and his newly found assistant Chet were at the house of the Lt. Col., a portly man, who had been retired from the army following the revolution of 1950. As was, however, usual, this particular individual had not been particularly affected by the new order of things. Firstly, prior to 1950, his attendance at army functions had been nominal, now it was non-existent. He had not been ostracized, for a lot of the C class Ranas, like himself, had been so affected. Now these things did not matter, and furthermore, because of the fact everyone was related to everyone because of the closed community in which marriages took place, everyone was happy with the status quo.

The Lt. Col. was glad to see Bir and Chet, not because of their presence in their indivudual capacities, but because of the birds that the two had brought. The same cocks fighting one another every week or so, as if it was a league championship, was boring. What was needed was some new blood for some real 'knockout' fights. The question was, would these two birds provide it?

The Lt. Col. got one of his birds and pitted it against the one which Chet had been carrying. The red scraggy bird under Chet's care would be, one thought, no match for the much heavier built one of the Lt. Col. The fight started, the two cocks faced each other, beak to beak and their crests stood on end. The heads moved up and down a little, in unision, each cock looking for an opening to get the upper or real clout. The scraggy bird managed to hold the bigger cock's beak, raised itself above the ground and gave a hefty kick. The bigger cock stood its ground and the too obvious example was a though a fly had kicked at an elephant. The bigger bird was, however, rather slow for the scraggy one and it was the latter's agility which in fact seemed to be the deciding factor. After a little while, however, the Lt. Col. turned to Bir Bahadur and said, "Let your other bird have a try at my one too. Your number one bird, though fast, will really have to put some thrust into its kicks, if it is to achieve anything against my bird."

Bir felt the blood rushing up to his face for he was sure that his bird was the better one. He motioned to Chet to pick up the first bird and then taking his other game cock he went and put it in front of the Lt. Col's bird. The birds started in real gusto, and because this second bird of Bir's was bigger, it was obvious in no time at all that the Lt. Col's bird was getting a thrashing. The bird's plight was obvious and before it could turn tail, the Lt. Col. said, "I think that my bird is a little tired now seeing that it has fought twice. Your birds have had a try out, so we let them fight it out next week"

Bird did not say anything in reply. By next week he would have bigger and quicker birds. He would make use of all the tricks of the trade. There were after all hormones, amphetamines and other drugs about which the Lt. Col. did not know anything. Bir would show the Lt. Col. what his cocks were worth. Other fights, or rather work outs, then took place and finally the dispersal for the morning.

When next week came the cocks started fighting again. Bir Bahadur realised that his outlook was not the fight, nor the possibility of antagonising the Lt. Col. by winning over his birds. Bir's intention was to use the Lt Col. as stepping stone to success. There were bigger and better things at stake. This realisation came when he went to buy some local cocks at Thaiti, for Bir's intention was to try to train these too for fighting, although he had heard stories to the contrary, for example, that these locals were not of much use as fighters. During his and Chet Bahadur's walks in Thaiti, they saw quite a few of the Managis carrying bags and also thermoses in their hands. Bir wanted to buy one but was told that they were sold in bulk to the local dealers in Juddha Road in Kathmandu. Bir and Chet stuck behind the Manangis and followed them first to the various shops in Asan, and Kamaladi and finally to Juddha Road. Snippets of conversation came through to

Bir during the course of these wanderings.

"This time you don't seem to have brought much in the way of goods. Is it due to the new regulations ?"

"Yes, you know during late King Mahendra's time they used to allow us to bring goods upto Rs. 10,000 after one months residence abroad plus an extra Rs. 3,000 worth of personal stuff. Well that period is all over. We people from Manang are not given so many privileges. Now there is just a blanket rule for everyone – Rs. 3,000 for all."

"That still does not explain the fact that some of this stuff does not look quite clean. Where did you pick it up ? In Singapore, Bangkok or Hong Kong, or on the pavements of Taiwan?"

"This time I was at Gelang in Singapore and then also at Phorat in Bangkok. With the new changes in Laos and Cambodia, there is now no question of going there. Furthermore with the ceiling of Rs. 3,000 it hardly seems worthwhile to go all the way to Hong Kong."

The shopkeeper persisted with his queries. "Why don't you get some drugs like prednisolone, or cyanocobalamine or even tetracyclines ? The market in India is almost a bottomless one. It is just that we cannot supply what is wanted."

"None of this drug stuff is available in Hong Kong or Singapore. I can however get you Seiko watches from these places."

After the Manangis had finally disposed off their goods, and were on their way back, Bir and Chet approached one. They got talking and it turned out thar he was a Gurung—a certain Dorji Gurung and lived in Thaiti in the vicinity of Kathe Simbhu. As they entered the compound of Dorji's house, Bir and Chet realised that they were in a community of the Manangis. There was a whole lot of them, sitting cross legged on the lawn and playing what seemed to be some sort of dice game. The little cup with the dice was brought down with a slap to the ground and then each of the participants gave a loud guffaw. On the outer fringe of this group, there were some toddlers, minus their trousers, running about here and there. A couple of these kids were biting away at a piece of dried meat, as they moved from one end of the compound to other. As the two went up the stair hard on the heels of Dorji Gurung, they realised that the house apparently had quite a few families of Managis there.

Dorji Gurung had a biggish room on the first floor of the house. The room was homely, with the numerous dragon-embroidered carpets on the floor and dragon carved and ornately coloured Tibetan tea tables along two sides of the room. In the corner near the door was a huge cardboard box with rolls and rolls of cloth, presumably saris of various bright colours. On the wall, at the far end of the room, was a glass cupboard within which were images of Tara, Sangechebame, Sangejibmiyang and Sangechomdung. In front of these were a row of small electric candles. The room was heavy with the odour of the jasmine scented incense sticks burning at that end. As they sat down Dorji rather apologetically informed Bir and Chet that as this was a place of warship, he would request them not to smoke here. He went on to inform the two that this was not the only restriction, as one was not allowed to bring meat in there, too.

Between cups of the salted and buttered tea with milk, Bir and Chet talked about the possibility of joining forces to do an import export sort of business. "I think that there is great scope in this. I have got some financiers on hand, if what I have is not enough. I am also getting in touch with people who will be able to afford us some protection if it is ever required," said Bir.

"We can give it a try. If it works, well and good; if it doesn't then we will just disband. I can't however be the only

Manangi involved. I would like to have a friend of mine, called Pemba Gurung with us."

Bir had no objection and so a preliminary plan was drawn up regarding the future course of action.

One particular morning, when they had got to Dorji Gurung's house they found him just making preparations for worship – a daily ritual which lasted for about ten minutes and which had been a part of Dorji Gurung's life from the time that he had been a small boy in the cold, inhospitable wilderness of Manang. The ritual started with the cleaning of the twenty-one small, aluminium bowls and the pouring of a little water into each. Then the two cup-like utensils at each end into which Dorji put in some rakshi. Finally the pouring in of oil and the placing of a wick in a central container which was then lighted together with the incense sticks. Dorji Gurung had been during all this time muttering his prayers, but now he came and sat down with Bir and Chet. He had finished his ritual for the morning: and the light and the incense sticks would burn the whole day, till it was evening time, when it would be time to existinguish it, and throw away the water and the rakshi in the little containers.

During the course of the next month, Bir and Chet worked out with Dorji and Pemba all the particulars about what they were going to take out of Nepal and what they were going to bring in. The contacts with the Lt. Col. being no less important, were continued by the simple expediency of Bir and Chet being regulars at the Saturday morning cock-fights. One day, after the morning's fights were over, the Lt. Col. invited Bir and Chet for tea upstairs. From cock-fights the talk turned to army days and it was no wonder that Bir and Chet also started dropping in almost daily to the Lt. Col's house. The talks then went on to about Burma, Thailand and Singapore and Bir almost casually dropped the information about the tremendous fortunes to be made in this line. The Lt. Col. was all ears in his enthusiasm, offered to take Bir to meet a certain General. The pros and cons of the proposed business were gone into throughly, and finally the General let it be known that he too was interested. It was decided to start a firm and then to go in for import and export via Bangkok and Singapore, then also via Burma for gems and drugs on the quiet.

10

The Gurkha Impex Company was formally started with about six shareholders. The front man was, of course, Bir Bahadur who now had substantial funds, from the accounts of the various Marbaris who had asked him to bring the money across, plus also from the last windfall, viz. that of Garibi Mal who had been arrested in Burma. There was, of course another Marbari from Burma but he, being a Burmese still at that time, could not go back to Burma, but would have to take up new papers oı somehow take up Nepalese citizenship, which was now a cumbersome proces in that one had to show some parentral connection or fulfil requirements such as residence for a number of years. His name was Chotu Ram Aggarwal; at least this was his original name, his Burmese name which he had once used in the hope of getting favoured treatment being now a forgotten thing. Then there was the General, a certain Gorkha Jung Bahadur Rana, who was their source of strength. In terms of financial contribution, the General's share was next to nothing, but in terms of profit it was understood that the spoils would be shared equally. Then there was also the Lt. Col., who went by the very impressive name of Victor Jung Bahadur Rana, for he had the privilege of being born on that day November in 1918 when the Allies had been victorious over Germany. There were also the Managis, Dorji Gurung and his frieud Pemba Gurung, who had one share each. It was a combination of convenience, two Ranas, two Manangis and the two Burmese expatriates. Chet Bahadur was also there, not as a member of that inner sanctum, but more as an assistant to Bir. Chet was quite happy, for not having invested anything he could not ask nor make demands, but the assurance that he would be a courier to and from Bangkok, Singapore and Hong Kong and the prospect of spending wonderful nights in those cities had left him in an anticipatory but placid state.

Within six months the firm, under Bir Bahadur or 'Lahure Dai' as he was sometimes referred to, was doing well. It was quite in order for him to travel via Shillong, to Imphal in Manipur and then into Burma. The fact that he was fluent in Burmese helped considerably, and he was thus able to get along inside the country without arousing any suspicion. The first time that Bir—'Lahure Dai' got there was very illuminating and an event in itself.

It did not take long for Bir to find out that the big boss of this area of the 'Golden Triangle' on the borders of Burma, Thailand, Laos and China was a man who everyone referred to as Big Kim. It was rumoured that Big Kim knew everyone and everything that took place in the Golden Triangle. Not only that, Big Kim was a man with a history, having entered Burma some thirty years ago as a member of the 93rd Division of the Koumintang Army hotly pursued by the Communists. Bir Bahadur spread the word around that he was keen to meet Big Kim. The villagers said that he would have to wait for a couple of days, for the following day was the important 10th of October, a day the Koumintang diehards celebrated. This Bir readily believed for he had noticed in and around a couple of small houses various coloured buntings and perhaps flags of the old Nationalist regime of China.

Two days later a man came along and said that he was an emissary of Big Kim and that Bir was to go along with him. Bir suspected that it must be to one of the strongholds of Big Kim that he was being taken, for it was only after passing through numerous checks and various manned posts that they finally reached the core of the unit. This was not only a complete arsenal for the underground army but there was also the various paraphernalia associated with heroin refining —large bottles of chloric acid, large tins of either, adequate stores of ammonium chloride and various other chemicals.

The man in charge of the factory was a man called Koh. After the usual introduction, Koh said, "Look, as far as we are concerned you can take some of the No. 3 or the No. 5 heroin with you this time, or if you like you can have the red stuff known as 'red chicken'. To tell you frankly, however, the market in the United States is what we are after. Your proposal to get the stuff to Kathmandu and then out does not interest us. It is a much easier proposition to get the stuff to Bangkok and then to Europe via Amsterdam."

"The market is developing. We have got quite a few hashish takers in the hippie community at Kathmandu. They could be used as couriers," said Bir.

"The more trouble then. Anyone can recognise these hippies anywhere. Then moment the customs people in any place on earth see that one is from Kathmandu, I believe that they really give him or her the third degree treatment. No, I am sorry, your proposition does not really interest us."

Having been given the cold sholder shoulder by Big Kim's group, Bir decided to go and visit his wife Way Shin Yi's brother Myu Myin Chi. The first place that Bir went to look was at Taunggyi, the heart of the Shan country at the fruit orchard where his brother-in-law had been the manager. Then through various contacts. It was therefore sometime later that Bir was able to locate him, and it was but a natural occurence for Myu Myin Chi was then in the SSA or the Shan State Army. Bir found him resting in a jungle camp dressed in the traditional Bantai or Shan lungi. When Bir told him about the talk with Koh, the latter said, "Look Bir, why do you want to buy the refined stuff? I can let you have quite a bit of the opium the next time after we have ambushed one of Big Kim's convoys of mules on its way to the factory. But again it is the question of market for what can be got out of Kathmandu is peanuts. The real market is in the West—the risk is there, but so also is the money."

In the end it was the Shan insurgents, fighting for their constitutional right of secession, who suggested to Bir that he should not restrict himself to opium or heroin but rather diversify. Plenty of people were doing this sort of activity—bringing articles such as cosmetics, etc., from Thailand and selling it to the people in the black market. It was a known fact that most of the women and the men were carrying small items in the hollowed out core of a thanaka wood piece. A simple ploy which was sure to succeed, provided, of course, that one had made some sort of arrangement with the people at the border. Amongst the other items, there was first of all the soft and pure gold from Thailand which had been brought through Chantu. Then came rubies, jade, the rare coral-like mogok, which had given the place its name and the blackish chowme. Then there were the images of Buddha, which the insurgents were willing to let him take and sell to the outside world via Kathmandu. The precious and semi-precious stones, jades and images to the curio dealers; and narcotics to the underworld at Kathmandu suddenly made this a very profitable business. Of course the other more legitimate side, the import of cosmetics, polyster wears and textiles from Taiwan, Hong Kong, Bangkok and Singapore all played their part in making their balance sheet presentable.

This more legitimate side of the business was looked after by the Managis Dorji and Pemba Gurung. They would take herbs, carpets, khukuris and other curios with them to Bangkok, Singapore and Hong Kong. There was also the so called 'Gall of the Bear' or 'Bear's Bile' which in reality was the bile of the buffalo, but was nevertheless in great demand as an aphrodisiac. All this of course meant that both Dorji Gurung and Pemba Gurung would be away separately for periods of upto a month, come back to spend a few days and then go off on their jaunts again. Whilst away from Nepal. in whatever city they happened to be in, they would buy semi-precious stones in the local market, and sell it later at a profit as the genuine stuff from the Himalayas. It was a hard life, however, for it meant an early start at 7.00 a.m. at the market-place, then the whole day would be spent with the goods spread out on the footpaths of the bazaar and finally, to round it off around the cinema halls, till about 11.00 p.m.

On first sight therefore, it was a wonder that only a year after it was started the Gurkha Impex Company had gone into liquidation, and lo! another, the Chamri Impex Company, had taken its place. It was all necessary to save some of the profits from the tax people.

Chet Bahadur was a companion to Bir not only in his business but also in his women hunting forays. Though they both received their sexual gratification in these outlings, Chet knew that Bir was not happy. Initially it was the thought of his Burmese wife. Later Bir found through an intermediary, during the course of one of his trips to Burma that Way Shin Yi had cancer of the breast and was receiving treatment for the same. Hearing this Bir was dejected for months afterwards, but having by now managed to get Nepalese papers and a Nepalese passport, Bir felt that it would be foolhardy to claim or state that Way Shin Yi was his wife. He could, however, with impunity take the regular Union of Burma Airways flight via Calcutta to Rangoon. He did not dare to speak any Burmese on the plane.

Bir's flight to Rangoon was uneventful but once he he got there and stepped out of the plane, he felt dejected. It was not the Burma, in fact not the life and the atmosphers, that he knew. There was the tropical heat and the eternal drizzle of rain, but it did not comfort him for he had not brought along an umbrella. The Rangoon that Bir remembered had been quite colourful. True, the standard wooden Rangoon suburban house was still built raised above the ground, but the grass growing everywhere, and the lack of paint made all the difference. This depressing picture was made worse as he looked arount the road to the Beach Palace Hotel. This hotel, which was by the river, had seen better days when the British were there. As one entered the hotel one did see some paintings of Burmese girl dancers, and the air of the old colonial legacy still hung around. Bir remembered the story about the conquest of Burma. It was, as vaguely remembered, just a question of shoes which had led to the downfall of the monarchy. What were the old sayings ? 'A Shoe is lost for want of a Nail', 'My Kingdom, my kingdom, my kingdom for a horse'. It wasn't the horse's shoe but the shoes of the British resident at Mandalay which had brought this about. The story went that the resident had complained that he had had to take off his shoes in the presence of the king, but had subsequently been instructed by the then Government of India in 1885, not to comply with the rule in future. The king of Burma was also adament in his refusal to meet the British resident as long as he was loth to take off his shoes in a kiug's presence. This led to a number of wars, the annexation of Burma, and finally to the abolition of the monarchy.

This was the Burma that Bir had known, the Burma of the British, and that of the old post Independence days. The present day Rangoon did certainly seem different from the the Rangoon of those days. True. it was the same Rangoon in the sense that it was the same city located on the Rangoon river some twenty-one miles from the sea. When Bir walked aronnd the wharf, there seemed to be guards at every corner, pointing their guns in every conceivable direction. Bir walked the Rangoon streets. These too had changed. The uneven pavements with its puddles of water, the broken covers of the blocked drains, which no longer seemed to function, made walking hazardous. And then there were the beggars-mostly lepers with their disfigured faces or their stubby fingers.

Another sign of the British legacy was the various

crudely hand-painted small signboards inviting one to have English correspondence or other matters typed by the typists' pool. There was not much to window-shop, for most of the windows were empty. The old pavement pedlars were there, but they seemed more ragged and without life. The zest had truly gone. There were the usual items—plastic dolls, fountain pen, cigarette lighters and cakes of soap sold also by girls who would have looked vastly different inside a shop. Here they sat on little stools, with their wares on a tray placed on their knees or on a small table in front. Their disenchantment with life seemed to be written on their passive faces or denoted by the bored way in which they flicked through a cheap Burmese paperback. Then the fruit vendors trudging along carrying the fruit in wicker baskets suspended at the two ends of a shoulder poll. Resting wearily from time to time in this process of making a meagre living, they walked on in spurts and jerks. During this process the hand of a bystanding rickshawallah would deftly dart forth and quickly remove a fruit from the basket. The poor man's load was lighter but his profit was gone—a day to day reality in the strange world of the Burma of today !

It was thus apparent at once that all said and done there was a shortage of goods and it seemed that whenever one required anything, one had to go into the queue and get it, or pay the exorbitant black-market prices. The artificially created shortage and the middlemens' profit, meant that the cost of everything was virtually ten-fold at the unofficial black rate. This was nowhere more apparent than in the official and non-official rate for the dollar—offically 6.50 Kyats, but unofficially upto 25 Kyats per dollar. This was confirmed after a reasonably short taxi-ride, when Bir gave the driver one green dollar, and received back fifteen Kyats.

Realising now how cheap taxis were, Bir hailed another one and asked the driver to take him around the town. He was shown the Shwedagon and the other pagodas. What the taxi driver was, however, keen to show Bir, was the new and well known Kareweik 'hotel'. This hotel called after an imaginary bird, was in fact a floating' restaurant on piles at the lake's edge. It was constructed in the shape of a Burmese King's royal barge and had been completed in 1972. From there the taxi driver took him to the gigantic reclining Buddha that was still under construction. The colossal figure made Bir think and refiect that the Burmese perhaps laid more stress on religion than the Nepalese did. Bir realised then that during all his years in Burma he had taken all this as a matter of fact

Back in the Beach Palace Hotel in the evening, Bir realised that it was half empty. True, the doorman at the front gate spoke a semblance of Nepali but Bir still did not feel quite at home. This hotel which had seen better days now seemed out of place here. Bir gazed at the mellowed crockery - Derby china had been probably ordered when the British were ruling Burma. Had they ordered so much that was still enough stock after more than a quarter of a century, or was it because the wear and tear or breakages were negligible becanse the hotel itself was in so little use ? Perhaps the latter reason, Bir thought. To him it appeared as if Burma was a nation withdrawing herself like a silkworm into her cocoon. When would they come out ? Would they ever come out ? He wondered.

The next day, Bir decided to take a train and visit Maymyo. A few hours by train and he was there. How the place had changed. There was the old Gorkha Road and the Durga Mandir, which, if he recollected correctly, had been made in the late fifties at the then fabulous cost of three lakhs of Kyats. It was still the hub of Nepalese activity at Maymyo, the place where they all met, where all the weddings, even upto five or six a day were held. There was still the old dharmasala and old 'Nepali' school. The latter, though now nationalised, still taught Nepali. Since all these changes were only too apparent, Bir now felt he was getting on in years.

He had the feeling that he ought to make a clean break with the past. There was no point in hankering for, or reminiscing about, it now !

On his return to Nepal, Bir had some sort of indirect information that his Burmese wife Way Shin Yi was dead. He felt sorry and dejected but at the same time he felt now that he had no duty to fulfil. He had a clear conscience on that score. He knew that this was exceptional for quite a few of the Nepalese and Indians had obligations there when they left Burma, and had intentionally deserted their wives and left the country to start life anew elsewhere. For Bir there was no question of claiming any property in Burma. Anything that his wife had, in the from of immovable property, would have reverted to the state. Bir decided to settle once and for all in Nepal now—his trips abroad or to Burma would now be strictly for business only.

Bir, however, still had some emotional attachment to Burma, and he was sometimes saddened by the thought of the existing conditions there. On the other hand, his euphoria knew no bounds when he thought of the Nepal which he had left formerly for greener pastures. The Nepal of today was a complete change—a true matamorphosis, which gladdened his heart. One day Bir confided to Chet all the troubles of his heart; and Chet, true to his ways assured Bir that his problems were now almost solved. It would be his job, his responsibility, said Chet, to find a girl for Bir.

Sure enough one fine day, Chet came around with the news that his latest girl friend, an air hostess in the RNAC had an elder sister, Janaki Tamang; who, for some reason, had not yet married though she was now about 30, and so might be a suitable match for Bir who was nearly 40 years old. Realising the fact that he was no young chicken, and what he wanted was a wife of child-bearing age, Bir readily consented. Their marriage was a simple affair and soon enough Bir had consummated the marriage in the hope that his first born child would be a son.

A year went by, then another, but still no result. Bir was getting worried. What was the cause? Was it the syphillis that he had contacted during the course of his stay at Calcutta that was the cause of all this? Was it the morning discharge, the gleet or the gonococcal infection of his epididymus, which was the cause of all this? Bir hawked his wife around all the lady doctors and even the male gynaecological specialists of Kathmandu. He did worship to Ganesh, at the temple of Anamatya Bhairab near the Pashupati temple, then at Attackh Narayan but still no result. He turned to the holy men and got various amulets from them all as a symbol of good luck, but to no avail. He had the holy scriptures recited, also a Navah, and got his wife to listen to everything.

Bir was, however, always getting his wife examined but never himself. The thought of masturbating to produce a semen specimen for the examination of sperms was just not only repulsive but absolutely abhorant to him. He was, after all, he felt, a man who always had a down to earth outlook on sex. He was certain that his sperm count was neither low nor of inferior quality. Bir therefore requested the doctor to try someting else and it was then agreed that Janaki would be given hormone injections, only if Bir agreed to have an examination of his semen. Before starting Janaki on the course of injections the doctor jokingly remarked that it was quite possible for her to get a whole lot of babies, like a litter of pigs. Bir remembered having read such items in the papers and retorted back, saying that he would be quite happy provided the doctors could ensure the survival of the little ones when they arrived. The news that it was he, Bir, who was at fault in that he was sterile did not bring any sort of shock or despondency that the doctor had anticipated. Bir had perhaps secretly suspected it all along but the news that it was the mumps which he had had as an adult and not the V.D. which was the cause of it, was something new to Bir.

The doctor gave Bir the news that the Family Planning Association Branch at Bhaktapur was conducting a marriage counselling clinic plus a clinic for childless couples. After making appropriate enquiries, Bir and Janaki made an appointment, and went there. They met the lady doctor, and she listened sympathetically to their tale of woe. She was, it seemed, conducting some research on artificial inseminations, and would be prepared to do so in their particular case. The lady doctor would insert the male sperms inside Janaki's uterus. She asked Bir if he had a donor, some close relative, or a friend, whom he could depend on for secrecy.

'I would leave the choice to you, doctor, for it is better that neither Janaki nor I know who the donor is. Unless it is anonymous, as far as we both are concerned, it is bound to lead to some psychological upset,' said Bir.

The doctor nodded and called out, "Kaley ! Kaley !"

A scruffy looking man who want by the name of Kaley because of his dark complexion entered the room. This man was in fact the peon but everyone referred to him as 'Kaley the Palle.'

"Kaley, I want you to have a look at this gentleman here. I want you to go to the local college, and look around for a Tamang boy of similar build and characteristics and approach him as a semen donor. You know the usual stuff. There will be the usual payment. The only thing I want you to make sure is that you don't tell who it is for. It might lead to complications between the mother and the donor." Kaley nodded instantly. Bir wondered if Janaki had understood all the conversation. Her face did not reveal anything.

The following week Bir and Janaki arrived for their appointment with the lady doctor, who did the artificial insemination of Janaki. All three waited for the next fortnight, and when Janaki missed her period, it was presumed that she was pregnant. When the next month went by, and she again did not menstruate, then it was virtually certain. To confirm, however, a urine test was done and when this was pronounced positive for a pregnancy, Bir's elation knew no bounds. Bir fussed over his wife; she had the best antenatal care that was available in the town. The rising expectations as the delivery date approached, the rush to the hospital, the waiting outside the labour wards for what seemed an eternity and then the actual birth of child. Bir heard the wailing cry of the child as it was born; but when no one came to give him the news immediately, he wondered if something was amiss. The nurse came after what aeemed and eternity and said in a matter of fact tone that Janaki had given birth to a little girl and that both mother and daughter were doing well. Bir tried to show some elation at the news but deep inside he was smarting from what seemed a mortal blow. If only that child had been a boy !

Before the little girl, who was named Pyari, was barely a year old Bir took Janaki to the Marriage Counselling Clinic at Bhaktapur and once again, Kaley the Paley contacted the young college boy for a specimen of his sperms. This time the boy demanded more, after all, he was the hope of this couple, who could not have a child of their own. Who knows, if it was again a girl, there would be still another occasion when they would try for a son to carry on the family, and to perform the funeral rites. Janaki became pregnant again and this time a boy was born. It was whilst the mother was still in hospital that the doctor sent for Bir and said, "I know how much you have waited, and to what lengths you have gone to get this son of yours. I have however some bad news for you. This child of yours is a Mongol."

"Well what is wrong doctor? As far as I know we Tamangs are said to be of mongoloid stock," said Bir.

"Sorry, my fault. I shouldn't have used that word. What

I suspect is that due to various signs, your new born son is what they call a case of Down's Syndrome. To come more down to earth, it means that your son will be rather behind others of his age. He will not be able to go to school like a normal healthy boy", the doctor quickly said.

Bir took all this with mixed feelings. As the boy grew, it was soon apparent that the doctor had been right. Bir felt depressed and then to let matters sort themselves out, decided to visit his Burma once again. The doctor's parting words were still ringing in his ears. "It is not the end of the world that this signifies. Your wife is still young and the fact is that this is a chance happening. I am sure that if you do decide to have another child, the chance of the baby being defective are not so great."

It was no trouble for Bir to get a Nepalese passport. His friends Dorji Gurung and Pemba Gurung seemed to know everyone of importance. It was therefore quite easy for Bir to take the Union of Burma Airways to Rangoon. It was 1973. Reaching there, Bir felt that what he wanted was some solitude to thlnk about everything, and sort out matters. What other place was there than Pagan, the City of Pagodas, or the Heart of Pagoda Land. After all, this was the place where people had literally been saving up gems and gold for Maitreya or the coming Siddhartha. Bir had been there years before and he remembered it as as a place without guards and with real gems lying all around the place.

There had been an earthquake Bir heard, but the area was not restricted to anyone officially. Bir decided to go there in as inconspicuous a state as possible. Ariving at Pagan, Bir asked a rickshawallah to take him to Shwezigon Pagoda where the frontal bone and a tooth of the Buddha were kept. Bir went there, and found that a few of the pagods had been destroyed in the quake. Then he remembered that some years ago he had seen the 'stapna' of the founding of a pagoda at

Mogok. A lot of the devotees, especially women had put in gold, rubies, diamonds and saphires in the core of the pagoda. Bir was convinced that it was just a matter of digging a little among these damaged pagodas, or simply searching about, that would enable him to strike rich by finding gems,

Bir got the rickshawallah to agree to come there in the night, by simply offeing him a liberal amount of green dollars. During the course of the night, the two working stealthily, managed to lay their hands on quite a few gems. By the next day Bir was back in Rangoon and ready to take off for the return to Kathmandu. It was on the plane that he heard about an Italian tourist who had gone to Pagan the previous week and having spent all his time there was on the point of leaving Burma to head back home. During the course of a routine search the customs people had found a tin full of precious stones which the tourist had stolen from Pagan. Bir kept quiet and prayed to Lord Buddha to protect him. How ironic it seemed—praying to the Lord from whom he, Bir himself had stolen.

When Bir arrived back in Kathmandu, he had visitors at his house. It was Kaley the Paley, from the Bhaktapur Marriage Counselling Clinic, and a young lad who said that he was Kipak Tamang, the father of Bir Bahadur's children. It transpired during the course of the conversation, that Kipak had during the past couple of months developed a friendship with Kaley and then got to scrummage around the files at the clinic. Having found the address of Bir and Janaki, the two had come with the intention of enquiring if further services were required to bear a son. Finding out that Bir was away, the two had hit on the bright idea of blackmailing Janaki. They threatened to tell the whole neighbourhood and make Janaki the laughing stock of the tole or locality. Janaki paid the hush money, whilst Kaley and Kipak were happy for they had adequate funds for drinking. Bir's initial impulse was to tell them to go to hell, but on second thoughts seeing that he now had brought enough wealth from Pagan, he decided that he would talk Kipak into providing his sperms and consequently his genes for yet another time. Of course Bir would pay him generously.

11

It was at the end of 1975 that Bir decided to revisit Deurali Chetrafal. A cadastral survey was going on and as he went towards Bhimdhunga during the early hours of dawn he met quite a few of the people who were coming back carrying big solid pieces of sakkar (molasses) in dokos on their backs. What a life he thought, as he saw these people with lighted flares in one of their hands whilst supporting the dokos with the other. There was at least some modernity about them for the flares that they were carrying were pieces of long polythene tubing—in fact tubing which was supposed to supply water to the rural folk. These pipes, indiscriminately hacked out at different sites, were truly community property which these portering individuals had utilised for their own needs. Had he not gone aboard, would he, Bir, have been like them, he wondered? Perhaps as a landowner he probably would have been growing the sugarcane and perhaps would have become the benefactor of these people, in so far as he would have been providing them with jobs. Would his reobtaining possession of the land, the land which his father had bought, bring about any difference in his life? After all he was now fairly settled –though with more troubles than he really cared to admit or even to talk about. Would this mean another headache?

When Bir reached the village green after having been on the road walking in a way reminiscent of his army days, he found that the cadastral survey team was at that time functioning from the school house. The reason for this state of affairs, Bir found out subsequently was that this being the time of the winter holidays, the school being closed, the place was empty. True, it was not much of a building—a small double storied hut with three small windows facing south to get not only enough air as ventilation but also enough sunlight to keep the place well lighted and warm. Bir wondered how they managed to run a school in this place—the two rooms of the hut could hardly accomodate the four classes of the primary school. He would have to come some other time to find all this out. Perhaps he could donate a substantial amount of money to the local village panchayat and get the school named after his father. It would be Bir's gesture to his old man for all that he had done. Bir had really never been able to reciprocate all his affection and care during his father's lifetime. How ironic that he should do this after his father's death!

Bir went up to the survey team and identified himself as Bir Bahadur Moktan. As he said his name, a teen-ager who happened to be within earshot, said to a friend, "He is one of those winter migratory birds. He has come here for his winter rations."

Bir felt like turning round and telling this long-haired youngster, who was well-suited and booted, that he, Bir had probably spent as much time in this place as this particular youngster. An old man sitting on his haunches, with a stick in one hand for support turned towards the youngster and said, "Bir Bahadur is no new comer here. He has been gone a good many years but he did come here once after the war, when his father was alive. He has come to claim what is rightfully his."

The youngster did not say anything. A few of the others looked up with interest at this man. Was he an intruder coming in to upset the quiet life of the village? The cadastral survey team asked him to produce the receipts that he had obtainrd for having paid land revenue. Bir had none, but what he did have was a copy of the Lal Mohur paper or grant of the land. On the basis of this, the cadastral survey team brought out the relevant map pertaining to what had been Sapkota's Hill, for it went by that name still, it seemed. The log-book was opened, and it then transpired that the previous pradhan panch, a man by the name

Kul Dhoj Singh had sold the land in small bits or holdings to various villagers and issued receipts for having paid the land rates. As the Nepalese saying goes it was 'A situation in which the cat is in charge of the milk' or was it a case of 'When the cat's away the mice will play'? Bir was not snre which was the more appropriate description for the present context.

The question now was whather Kul Dhoj Singh, who did not own any of the land, have any right to dispose off it. The crux of the matter was that the whole of the land had been claimed by some of the villagers, one of whom was the long-haired youngsther, and except for the wooded area of pines, which the survey team was not registering under anyone's name, all the land had been accounted for. Bir had now come, virtually to upset the apple-cart, and claim that the land was his. He too signed in the log-book and as he penned his signature it meant that the land which half a dozen villagers had bought from Kul Dhoj Singh was under dispute. Even in this early stage Bir could tell that quite a few of the villagers were for him; and though they did not come directly forward they met him quietly at the side, and said that his claim was justified.

It was now obvious then that there were two groups in the village, Kul Dhoj Singh and his caucus on the one side, and the rest on the other. Kul Dhoj Singh took a few of his followers to one side and started saying, "Look it is a case of the land to the tiller. Those who have their land under ploughs should own it. I tell you Bir Bahadur does not own any land within the four kilas (boundary pillars) that he says. He might perhaps own the space in the sky above this area and has come to claim it." Kul Dhoj's caucus gave a loud guffaw, and looked at Bir.

"Don't mind what they say. That group has virtually ruled this village for the past couple of years. They had come as panchas from amongst us but they were a self-centered lot who have managed to do very well for themselves. Funds for this, funds for that, and then the money we paid as rates have yet to be accunted for. No wonder the villagers turned against them and did not elect them, but they still have some sort of hold in that they can make things difficult for the individual. I think we had better send for the new Pradhan Pancha. He was here till about half an your ago, he must have gone to have his meal", said a wiry looking old man wearing a bailaclava cap on his head. As Bir turned towards him, Bir had a faint smile on his face for the simple reason that this villager seemed out of this world with his four-day stubbled face peeping out of the circular opening of the ballaclava helmet like cap.

Great was Bir's surprise when he saw walking towards him a figure which reminded him of his friend Fatteh. As the person approached nearer, Bir was virtually certain that this was no other than Fatteh his old friend.

"Why if it isn't old Aite ? I wouldn't have recognised you had I not heard whisperings that you had come back to Deurali Chatrafal after all these years. I had heard it said that you had come here soon after the War but that you had left suddenly for Burma. Well, well it's nice to meet one's childhood friends."

"You haven't done badly, Fatteh. I suppose that it was natural for you to follow in the footsteps of your father Tauke Tamang who was the village headman then. You are the Prachan Panch. A rose called by any other name is still a rose."

"Well, Aite. No, I suppose I had better call you Bir. Well, you are in a bit of a mess as far as your land is concerned. I and half the village know that it really belongs to you. The fact was that your father and brother having died, your sister and you being away, the land had no one to claim or look after it for many years, and so it has apparently become common property, and had been turned into a gaucharan or the common village pasture land. A few more years, and other people had moved into it, of course with a bit of help from those who had a say in village matters. You make an application requesting that all attempts by others to register the land as theirs be declared null and void. I will try to sort it out at the village level, but I doubt if I will be successful: for all these people have paid money to those who hatched up this scheme. I think that you will perhaps have to go to court yourself, for I can't see them suing the ex-pradhan pancha."

As Bir and Fatteh exchanged words, quite a few of the villagers had gathered round. Members of the ex-prachan pancha's caucus realised that it was not going to be easy to deprive Bir of his ancestral property.

Fatteh continued: "Why don't you come and stay with me for a couple of days ? I am sure that there must be a lot of people you might want to visit or look up."

Bir nodded in assent, and then, after all the work with his land problem had been finished, he proceeded to Fatteh's place Bir had his meal at Fatteh's house and was just sunning himself in the afternoon sun, when Fatteh came back from a tour of the village.

"Look, Bir, the group is trying to discredit you now. They are trying to get the villagers against you by raking up the past. They probably feel that with me as prachan pancha they will not be able to say that the land which the ex-pradhan pancha sold belonged to him".

"What are they raking up from the past ?"

"I wasn't here but the story is that when you came here during one of your leave periods, you got yourself involved with the girl Sunu Maya. You led her up the garden path, got her pregnant and then abandoned her. After she had given birth to a boy, she is supposed to have committed suicide."

Bir did not say anything. He could not say anything. This was a bolt from the blue and it left him speechless, not because of what had happened, but because of the fact that he had been the cause of all these events.

"Fatteh, I won't deny that I was involved with the girl,

In fact I tried to talk her into coming to Burma wlth me but she refused saying that I would abandon her somewhere along the way. Furthermore when I did leave, I did not know that she was pregnant. Had she told me, or had I known, I would have married her there and then before I went off again. After all, it is quite customary for a lot of our folk to get married and then go ofl for a few years service in India, Pakistan, Malaya, Singapore, Borneo and Hong Kong. Then the other point is that if she was committing suicide because of the pregnancy, then she should have done so before the child was born."

"I don't think that we are in a position to decide that right now though I agree with you. I think, the best thing is for you and I to go to Tilak Bahadur Thokar, talk it over with him and then to sort out matters."

Their reception by Tilak Bahadur, Sunu Maya's father, was very civil. They talked about general matters before Fatteh brought up the question of Sunu Maya. He told Tilak Bahadur Bir's version of the story, which was basically that he, Bir, had not known anything about the pregnancy. Had he know, then he could certainly have married her.

It was a bit of a surprise to both Bir and Fatteh when the old man replied. "I bear you no ill will, Bir Bahadur. My daughter had your child and I think most of the villagers guessed and knew the facts. I toyed with the idea of even giving him your surname Moktan, but then gave it up for it would have meant more publicity of the fact that you and my daughter were 'blood cousins'. Hence I called him Top Bahadur Thokar, but he too knows the whole story, except the name of his father.

"Coming back to Sunu Maya, it was the illness after the pregnancy which carried her off. About a month or so after the child was born, she seemed to be a changed person. Rambling away, talking about very bizarre topics and images, and, above all, being at times very depressed and sad and at others excited and virtually maniacal. It was a problem trying to keep her indoors. I got our Jhankri Ba to try his methodss of excorcism, and he cut many cockrels, and even a black goat to appease the Devi at Bhatbhatini, but to no avail. One evening Sunu Maya gave us the slip and went out of the house. We found her soon enough. She had gone towards Kathmandu, but at the Thado Dando she had gone down the slope, right to the bottom. There was a big camphor tree there, which was fairly easy to climb. It was on this tree that she had hanged herself with her patuka. Her corpse was seen dangling on the branch the very next morning by the travellers on the bridle path. We didn't bring her back. We cremated her there. The big tree was not cut down but only the branch on which she hung herself. The tree is still standing. I would like to do a saptah for her there. It will help to free her soul and get her to heaven.

"Now only this morning a group of people came to see me with the intention of getting me to denounce you. I told them that I would do no such thing, but would rather let my daughter's soul rest in peace. I can't get over the fact that it is Kul Dhoj Singh who is trying to play the part of saint, and become the champion of the people. I can't forget the troubles that he used to create for us from time to time. I told them that matters regarding Sunu Maya are now a closed chapter of my life. They were a bit disappointed but went their way. So, Bir Bahadur, as far as I am concerned, you have made your peace with me. It is for you to get in touch with Top Bahadur in London and to come to some sort of understanding with him. How he will react, I don't know, for he was always a strong headed chap.

"However Top Bahadur has done very well and I am really proud of him. At the end of the training at Sandhurst, he was judged the best cadet. From what I can gather, he is going to be there with his battalion for some time to come. This does not upset me, for he has after all his own life to lead.

He is doing what he thinks is best for his future career. As for me I am quite content to spend the little time I have left, living quietly in our village of Deurali Chetrafal."

Fatteh and Bir took their leave of the old man and went back greatly pleased. The move to discredit Bir had been stopped before it had even started. Fatteh's feeling was that Bir would probably get his land, but that he would perhaps have to go to court to regain his rightful possession.

12

Top Bahadur was an industrious lad. Not only that, even as a child he excelled in almost everything that he did. It was no wonder, therefore, that during his days at Hong Kong with the 6th Gurkhas, he had been picked out as a promising lad and sent, with four others, to the military academy at Sandhurst.

Top Bahadur had heard so much about Sandhurst, but when he got to the place it was a bit of an anti-climax. After all Sandhurst itself was but a small village and the Royal Military Academy with its world wide reputation, was its only prize possession; but this fact did not lessen the pride which Top and his four companions felt, as they went through the doors of the Grand Entrance and into the heart of the Academy itself.

He and his mates were taken to the New College across the square. Tne vast red brick structure was not very new, but the traditional reference had been retained over the years. In it there were gentlemen cadets, they found, from not only England but from all over the world. Here was the institution thriving on its reputation, for all these cadets had come to do the Standard Military Course at Sandhurst.

It was during this time that Top came across some other boys who had also come there from Kathmandu. These boys had had been sent by the Nepalese army. There was a certain amount of rivalry between this group of two and Top's group of five. The Kathmandu boys had at first kept a little apart from the lads coming from Hong Kong, but whether it was because they considered themselves to be a class above them, he did not know; though it was a fact that they had more money to spend. It was therefore no wonder that the boys from Kathmandu always seemed to make a bee-line for London almost every Saturday or whenever any leave period came up. They seemed more adept at the good life, and though Top Bahadur did not approve of their ways at times, there came a period when with proximity, and growing familiarity the two groups came to regard themselves as one, and basically Nepalese.

Of the two boys, one was called Madan K.C. He was a good mixer not only only in the little group of Nepalese, but also amongst the other cadets. The fact that his surname was abbreviated to just initials K.C. was at first an object of universal curiosity, but Madan true to form, showed remarkable one-upmanship when he said that he was a Knight Commander. It was Madan K.C. who was always carping to the five lads from Hong Kong about offering their services to fight for a foreign army. "Quite frankly, I don't see what you boys joined up for. After all, I am sure that when you are in the British Army and have to fight, its not and cannot ever be for your own homeland," said Madan.

"So what. It's a job like any other. If doctors and engineers can go to foreign lands and earn money, they are also working as mercenaries. When such town-based educated elite decide to settle elsewhere, they are deserting their motherland. Why should people like you pick on us poor blighters from the hills and point you fingers at us ? After all there are not enough jobs to go all around, and by joining the British or the Indian Army, some Nepalese lads are at least bettering themselves and prehaps ensuring that they will be able to provide a better future for their families," replied Top Bahadur.

The Kathmandu boys in their turn, had also realised that as far as the army life was concerned, the boys from the hills who had come to Sandhurst via Hong Kong had a more healthy attitude and certainly were more professional.

They had initially tried to boss them, but when they realised that the five could not care less for them, they had given up teasing. Then there was also the fact that as far as sports were concerned the five as a group always had one or two of its members in any team. It was not just the usual sports such as football, hockey, basketball and swimming but even a so far unknown sport such as rugby. Then there was pugilism or, as some said, the noble art of self defence, or boxing. After this the Nepal Cadets had taken to the Hong Kong batch and had seen to it that this group also came into contact with the other Kathmandu boys, or other Nepalese professionals, who were working or studying in London. It was through these two boys' efforts that the Nepalese Embassy officials invited these expatriate Hong Kong lads to the embassy parties on the occasions of Dasain and the King's Birthday.

Top Bahadur had found the parties that he attended rather interesting The fact that he met so many Nepalese, and heard their views on the present day Nepal, was an eye-opener in the sense that he realised that the people back in Kathmandu were doing their level best to try to get the country moving and developing at a rapid pace. Some of the boys had tried to get him to join the Nepalese Students' Association known as 'Yetis', but he and his comrades had shied away from this, saying that as they were army personnel, they would not involve themselves in such social engagements.

After completion of the standard military course, Top Bahadur and his friends shifted to the Old College to do the regular career course. This course being less rigorous than the basic one, meant that they had more time to take part in the various extra curricular activities at Sandhurst.

When Top Bahadur had almost finished his two year stint at Sandhurst and looked forward to being a 2nd Lt. with his brigade at Hong Kong, he suddenly heard that his battalion was coming to Britain, and that he would join them there. Top

Bahadur was happy. His days at Sandhurst, now almost at their end, had been marked by achievements. A notable all round sports activity, including the highlight viz. the receiving of the Queen's Sword for the best cadet. Then finally the day dawned when the Sixth Gurkhas came to the United Kingdom to make the Jellabad Barracks, at Tidworth, their temporary home.

To him and his other five comrades who had by now been well acclimatised in England, it was not much of a problem getting used to the life in the barracks out there;· but to their friends newly come from Hong Kong it was a very luxurious life. Then Top remembered the day of the family outing to Richmond Park one particular day. The walk through the woods, the fallen leaves on the ground and the sighting of the deer lolling about, had all reminded them very much of their own forests,

It had been a pleasant outing, and they had returned to their barracks in great spirits when suddenly there had occured a virtual catastrophe—people all over the barracks had developed diarrhoea and vomiting, and had to be rushed off to hospital. It then transpired that during the course of their afternoon stroll through Richmond Park, quite a few of the ladies, seeing the toadstools had mistaken them for edible mushrooms, and had taken them home to cook in the barracks. It was no surprise therefore that there had been an outbreak of food poisoning all around. Luckily, all had recovered after the prompt medical attention they had received.

Then the crowning achievement came at the time of the Army rifle meeting at Bisley, in southern England. The Sixth Gurkhas won on overall performance with rifle, pistol and machine gun. Not only that, Top Bahadur came top in the individual performance, and won the Army Medal.

Then arrived the day when the Sixth Gurkhas had to start providing the personnel for the Tower of London. It was thus that one fine day Top Bahadur found himself assigned amongst the guards there. It was a pleasant change from the day to day foot-slogging that he would have had to do at the barracks. Here he had to almost stand still for long periods, or supervise or direct the crowds from time to time. It was always a motley crowd there and he must have had his picture taken, God knows how many times. Then there were the Britishers who had served with the Gurkhas, who came up and said a word or two to him. Lastly there were the occasional Nepalese visitors to U.K. who came more to the Tower as sightseers.

It was in the midst of this whilst he was at the Tower that he received a letter addressed to Second Lt. Top Bahadur Thokar, Sixth Gurkha Rifle, Tidworth. From there it had been sent by army dispatch to him at the Tower. Top Bahadur wondered as he opened the letter as to who it could be from. Inside was a short slip saying that there was a long letter from Bir Bahadur Moktan, explaining certain things. The note was not signed but the writing was purportedly his grandfathers. He then turned his attention to the next letter. It went:—

Dear Top Bahadur,

I do not know how I should start this letter for the simple reason that I have never seen you, nor have you seen me. The fact that both of us are just blank faces, to each other, without any facial characteristics will I suppose help me in saying what I want to say.

The fact is that I am your father. I was the man who was involved with your mother Sunu Maya Thokar. We were attracted to each other, it was just a moment of passion when we made love for the first time and then again and again. Though there was further involvement we realised that we could not marry in the village because of our being 'blood cousins. I asked her to come with me to India for I was then willing to give up my army commission but she refused thinking that I would leave her once I got to India.

So I went back alone to Burma, thinking of her all

the time. When I came back to Nepal in the early fifties, I wanted to go to Chetrafal Deurali in Dhading, but the events at that time took such a sudden and unexpected turn that I could not go there to find out about your mother. It was only last year, in 1957, that I managed to get to the village and heard all about her. I felt guilty about her, about the fact that it was because of me that she took her own life. I met your grandfather Tilak Bahadur Thokar who told me all this, and also the fact that you are her son. I have made my peace with him and, I hope also with the soul of your mother Sanu Maya for I have done a Saptah, at the exact place that your mother died. So, my son, forgive me, accept me as your father, and I will to stand by you. I know it is a little late in life for me but I can try to make amends, which I greatly desire, and am still able to do, in expiation of my sins.

Your grandfather has been telling me of all your achievements. Your proficieney in all that you have taken up to do has not only surprised us but made us feel most proud of you. Not only grandfather and myself, but a whole lot of us Ex-service men, nay, the whole village, is proud of you. If fact, I do you injustice when I write this, for a substantial number of us Nepalese felt equally proud when they, and we read of your achievements in the local paper. We all look forward to the day when you will come home on your next leave. We will certainly give you a hero's welcome.

Please drop me a line, care your grandfather. I meet him often enough.

Yours ever,
Bir Bahadur.

As he read the letter, Top Bahadur's eyes became misty. It was not due to thoughts of his father, a man whom he had never seen but rather because this letter had woken up memories of a mother who had given birth to him and who he must have seen during the first month or so of his life. His grandfather had told him that his mother had commited suicide about a month or so after he was born.

Top Bahadur's first inclination was to tear this letter into a thousand shreds and throw it into the W.C. It was where it rightly belonged! Not only the letter, but also the writer, a man who claimed to be his father! On second thoughts, however, Top Bahadur decided to keep it and so taking out a note-book from his uniform pocket, he placed the neatly folded letter in the small note-book and put it back.

Although Top Bahadur tried to ignore the letter and its writer, inspite of him it became a letter which he read almost every day. The folds of the paper became thin and tattered, and in course of time he knew the entire contents by heart. Nevertheless the taking out of the letter and reading it became a daily routine, so much so that it was now an obsession.

Then one day a second letter arrived. It was not a direct letter, for there was a covering note from his compauy commander, saying that he Top Bahadur, was to go and see him the following week.

This second letter read:—

Dear Top,

I had written you a letter some time ago but since I did not get a reply, I thought that you did not get it. Perhaps it is our inefficient Post Office which is to blame. Consequently I am writing this letter care-of your company commander, and the same is being posted in London by someone who is going there for a few days. Also enclosed is a copy of the letter which I first wrote. I have also taken the liberty of sending a copy of this letter to your company commander in the hope that he will understand the situation and grant you something like compassionate leave to come back here for a month or so.

Well son, it is simply this. I have not got much longer to go in this life. I want to make amends and let you have all that I possess. You are my son, my one and only son, and it is you who will have to do my final rites when I pass away. It might be any day, so please hurry home. Once I have seen your face, and know what a handsome brave son you are, I can make preparations to meet my Maker. Any time after that 'Come, Tomorrow', and I shall be ready.

So son, come home, come, tomorrow ! I shall await for you.

Yours affectionately,

Bir Bahadur.

This time Top Bahadur felt the blood rush up to his face. His ears felt hot. They must be red he thought. What a foolish old man was Bir Bahadur ! And selfish too. All that he seems to want him back home is to perform his funeral rites. This seems to be the whole of the eastern temperament !

Top Bahadur took out the first letter, plus the copy of it and the second letter-and tore all these up into tiny shreds. His mind was now made up. He would never go back now.

The following week when Top Bahadur went and met his company commander, the latter asked him if all his problems had been solved.

"Yes, Sir, All solved. That is a closed chapter in my life."

"Don't you want to go there for some time now ?"

"You have been kind enough Sir, to suggest that I should go to see them. I don't want to go back. Never, Sir."

The company commander thought for a while. He did not want to be too involved in the family matters of his men, although as a Gurkha Officer he was much more involved in this sort of sorting out then for the average British private, he supposed. Well it was Top Bahadur's affair.

"That's all Top. I hope that you will recons decision for the sake of your old man. He must on in years. You may go."

'Thank You Sir,' said Top Bahadur, as he smartly saluted, about turned and marched smartly out of the room.

Top Bahadur's head was nearly bursting with all the thoughts that he had stuffed in it. He had to get it down quickly on paper and write to that fool of a father of his. He got to his room and set down to the task of writing.

Dear Bir Bahadur,

I received your letter in time, I had not replied for the simple reason that I was at a loss as to what to write to a man who says that he is my father and, whom I have not seen these last twenty nine years. The tone of your second letter has however put me off. I think you are a very selfish old man and that your only interest in me is that I continue your line, and perhaps do your funeral rites. As you wrote to me did you wonder as to who did these for Sunu Maya, my mother.

You write that you are all proud of me. For what? You have no reason to be. You have no right to be. It is misplaced pride. A Gurkha soldier wins the V.C., either posthumously, or, if he is lucky, alive. Why did he leave his home in the first place? Did you bother to think it might be due to the fact there was not enough to eat at home. That the family plot might be too small? That there might be no family plot? We had to go to as mercenaries, we had to sell our blood to get a chance in life. The British paid us and if you look at the history of the Gurkhas you will see that we have been in their service continuously since 1815, when the treaty for recruitment was signed. We have taken their salt, we have fought for them.

The attitude of some of our Nepalese countrymen has always been a source of amusement to me. I remember one particular party during Dasain. Everyone was a bit high then, and then one of your ministers turned around to our company officer, and said, "You know my soldier, your Queen's guard."

Our officer did not reply but just gave a smile. I could have given a mouthful, but I had to keep my place. I just thought that it is so typical of the Nepalese temperament, to take credit for acts which have been done by others.

As far as I am concerned, please don't bother about me any more. I will never come back to Nepal. I will serve in the British army until they either retire me or kick me out. Then I could join some force or security guard organisation in Singapore or Borneo. They pay well, I hear. So count me out of your life. I don't fit into your "Come, Tomorrow." As far as I am concerned I could not care less about you. You can go to Hell. As far as tomorrow is concerned, my sincere advise to you would be not to wait for it, for, your tomorrow will never come.

Top Bahadur

13

Bir Bahadur had looked forward to the letter from England, because he had been expecting an affirmative and loving reply. The contents, not the letter, had therefore been a bolt from the blue. He felt his life was falling to pieces; his wife was no longer his, his son was not interested in him, and the inheritance of his land was no longer assured. Finally his business was no longer going in the tempo in which it was won't to do. It was not a question of changing names from Gurkha Impex, to Chamri Impex, to what not Impex. It was something far more serious. The whole of the business was in the doldrums. A girl who was working for them, a certain Tschela, who was not only a cousin of Sonam Gyamzo but also an efficient courier had been arrested at the local Tribhuvan Airport. The funny thing was that it was not for the stuff that she had on her but instead for the measly three thousand green dollars that she had on her person. The payment of bail and getting her released was not the problem, for there were greater things involved. After all, they all knew she was carrying the stuff, they had known it all along, but had never bothered to make a fuss. It would have been impossible to get out of the airport at Bangkok, Singapore or Hong Kong if she had been just dependent on the one hundred dollars which was the amount officially allowed on her passport. It was now a question of principle. Why this sudden action? Was it a question of discreetly discouraging the deeds of the past? Were the sunny days when they used to be given plenty of lee way with the rope, over?

Having all these things on his mind did not help to give him peace. Chet Bahadur came to see Bir at his new quarters in

Jamal and found him very despondent. Bir Bahadur was very silent, and refused to talk. He was not the same man any more. and it was with a certain amount of coaxing that Chet Bahadur could get him to a local psychiatrist. The psychiatrist had a number of sessions with him and then on a certain day, he called Chet Bahadur aside and told him that his friend was suffering from an acute form of depression as a result of the break-up of marriage, and his other worries. Chet Bahadur, as his friend, would have to keep an eye on him, for in such a state anything was possible—even a suicide was possible. It could happen any time, for depressed people like Bir, did not usually talk about it. Chet Bahadur became very worried, and did not want to leave Bir to stay at Jamal and fend for himself. His worry was that Bir might decide to go and jump not in any lake but in the local water tank which was known as the Ranipokhari. This local water tank had been the most popular place for ending one's life among the local Kathmanduites. Chet Bahadur could not bear the thought of leaving him all alone and talked him into coming and living at the small hired apartment of Chet Bahadur at Thamel.

When Bir Bahadur did talk to him, he was very melancholy most of the time. Now it was about old age, and how with the changing way of life in the capital, the old people would have to start fending for themselves. The old family ways, with the extended family system was on its way out. He had had enough for his life-time. Chet Bahadur however, felt that the doctor had been wrong about his assessment of Bir. He felt that Bir would not commit suicide on two counts:-

1. Bir's nagging thought was that once he died there would be no one to do his argan of the annual ritual on the forty-ninth day of his death. This would lead to the fact that his soul would never get to heaven and that he would become a ghost in the nether-nether. Therefore Bir, also toyed with the idea of adopting someone for just this specific purpose.

2. The second problem would be about his young wife. She

had technically left him, but would her young lover leave her in the changed circumstances? Would he marry her—a widow? Suppose he left everything for his own son Top Bahadur? Would the latter take it, which would make life for his young wife even more precarious? Was it unlikely that Top would accept it? If Bir did adopt someone intelligent and resourceful as his dharmaputra or adopted son, then the latter would certainly not leave anything for his wife and the young lover. He felt that such action would certainly result in the lover Kipak Tamang leaving his wife and his two children. The thought of his wife's possible sufferings gave him a certain satisfaction but he decided against this in view of the little girl and the boy with the Down's Syndrome.

The diseased mind of Bir came up with a solution which he one day confided to Chet. It was simply that he, Bir, would go to his wife and her lover and make them a proposal. He would leave them everything that he had, provided that she had another son through her lover and said that the boy was his, Bir Bahadur's. Chet however was not so sure that this was so good an idea and decided to take Bir to the local Tri-Chandra Military Hospital to see the psychiatrist there and get his opinion. Bir agreed, and they went. Then the visit to the hospital, the cursory glance of the inscription at the top of the building which said, 'TRI-CHANDRA MILITARY HOSPITAL 1925 A. D.' and the sight of the statue of the soldier there, brought remembrance into Bir's mind. He remembered how some thirty-five years ago, he had entered the hospital to be examined by the doctors. There were the same words on the sides of the frontage of that building. Of course he had not been able then to read what it said. Now he read on one side the words, 'To the glory of Sri Pashupatinath and to the memory of those brave sons of the Kingdom of Nepal who fell in the Great War 1914-1918 A.D.' On the other side of the building frontage, the same sentiments were expressed in the Devanagiri script of Nepali.

How the place had changed ! The original building was there but some additions were evident. Small sheds like structures had sprouted all around like mushrooms. It was noticable that the present day hospital was providing treatment not only to the regular army, but also to their families and to ex-service personnel like him.

The doctor on hearing Chet Bahadur's account, and after examining Bir felt that the latter was a changed man—it was, he felt, perhaps a natural course of the disease. He gave some drugs and advised that Bir Bahadur go back to his own house and try to adjust himself to the atmosphere. Bir acted as advised, and found too that his wife and her lover Kipak now adopted a more sympathetic attitude towards him. In fact they got on very well, and then started having parties and inviting friends. It was however too good to last, and one evening the inevitable happened. Kipak got drunk and in that state started boasting about himself and then abused Bir Bahadur as an inadequate husband for Janaki. This was however too much for Janaki too, and she felt offended, and took the side of the old man Kipak now started ridiculing the wife too. Feeling that his presence there would only worsen matters, Bir turned and beckoned Chet to follow him and together they left the house for Chet's lodgings.

Bir Bahadur was still smarting from the words of abuse that Kipak had hurled at him during the course of the previous evening. There was no doubt about it, he definitely was a thorn in the side of Kipak. But would the same thing apply in his relationship with Janaki, his wife? He decided that he would spend the next few days at Chet's place, and wait, and see.

During the course of the first morning there, Bir unburdened all his troubles to Chet. The latter suggested that Bir should try to forget all these things, at least during this time of Dasain, the season of glad tidings and good cheer. Late in the afternoon Chet talked Bir into going around to the Tundikhel. How different it was when Bir had initially done his training there. Funny that he had not noticed the changes upto now, the cement railings around the famous parade ground had not just bisected, but even trisected it into three different enclosures. It was in the part adjoining the stadium that the shaggy mountain goats and the sheep from the Tibetan Autonomous Region of China and the long-eared, spindly-legged goats from the Bettiah region of India met to be sold to the Nepalese to make their Dasain merry. A real instance of good neighbourliness between countries if ever there was one.

By six that evening it was getting rather dark and chilly. Afters spending a couple of hours at Chet Bahadur's rooms at Thamel, the two decided that they would round off the day by paying a visit to Casino Nepal at the Soaltee Hotel. There was just the problem of them both being Nepalese, because the Nepalese were not allowed to play at the Casino. Was this an attempt to copy the customs of Monaco and the restriction on the Monagasques. It was not difficult however to get around this, for it was Bir who suggested, "Look, I have got a Burmese shirt, and after putting on lungi as makeshift sarong and tying a handkerchief around my head like a 'Gaungbaung', I can pass myself off as someone from Burma. You can then come as my guest. I think that we will be able to dodge the question of the passport by saying I left it at the hotel."

Hearing this Chet felt that Bir was now his usual self. Things were indeed looking up. "O.K. by me. You will have to play all the moves. It is only fair, seeing that you are going to be paying not only for your stakes but also for mine. You can play it in turns !"

They started walking. It was as if Bir was in Burma for as they walked, Bir would from time to time loosen his lungi, adjust and tuck it to his waist. This so fascinated Chet Bahadur that he remarked, "You looked so different all dressed up like this. Then the constant adjusting of the lungi. If you are frightened that it will come down and reveal you in your birthday suit, why don't you at least tie it up?"

Bir grinned and nodded his head as they hailed a taxi and asked him to make speed towards the Casino Nepal.

It was barely eight-thirty when they reached the Casino. The drive through the long driveway towards the hotel itself was not very impressive, for it seemed rather dark and it was as if they were going to a cloak and dagger encounter. The entrance to the Casino Nepal had two figures from a pack of playing cards painted on the glass door. It took some time to get in for just at that moment a whole coach load of tourists arrived on the transport which the management provided. As Bir and Chet reached there they could hear voices in various tongues, 'Kommen Sie ins Morgen',.......Manayana'. Bir deduced that some group was telling their driver to come perhaps on the morrow. If he could remember correctly, he thought that 'Manayana' probably also meant the same thing. So, these people were here to make it an all night session.

One of the visitors awaiting her turn to be registered and get her five dollars worth of free coupons saw a broken mirror on the wall and turning to the man at the top of the stairs said, "What is that for ? Does it mean bad luck for us and good luck for you ?"

"Oh No Maam, seeing that it is our mirror, we are in for bad luck. The good luck is all on your side," the young man said smiling broadly.

Bir seeing that he was in Burmese attire, played the part well even to the extent of whiffing a cheroot. As a Burmese, he picked up his sheet of five coupons—value of one dollar each for playing viz. Keno, Jackpot, Pontoon, Blackjack and Roulette. Chet filled a declaration saying he would not play.

The walls of the stairway leading down proclaimed the

present craze of the Kathmandu Casinoites. Chet and Bir Bahadur went down, and looked into a fairly big room with a roulette and a couple of card tables. It was empty and Chet was at a loss to understand; for a little further up there was the sound of bells ringing, proclaiming that someone had just hit the jackpot on one of the slot machines. Then Chet looked up and saw the reason, this was the hard currency area of the Casino, but somehow even the overseas tourists preferred the Casino atmosphere of the soft currency area and were more content to change their dollars for the chips of the rupee denominations.

The slot machines for the jackpot seemed fully occupied, but if the sounds of bells ringing was any indication, they were paying quite a bit. The two watched as an elderly lady with greying hair worked feverishly putting in no less than five coins at a time, to hit the jackpot. That she had hit a minor jackpot, if not the real thing, was evident from the pile of coins, which were almost to over-spilling point on her little plastic bowl and the small pan at the bottom of the machines into which the jackpot coins came trickling through.

The seats at the card and roulette tables seemed all occupied. The obvious thing to do was to change the Keno coupon and play. They went towards the counter and Bir changed his coupon for a sheet of the Keno game number four. Having picked their numbers they had to wait and so took the pontoon coupon to play at the table. One go and it was finished. The blackjack coupon fared no better, and so the obvious thing to do was to change their coupons into the slot machines coins and try. The free play coins finished and Bir now flushed to playing, changed another fifty. He won a few times and lost at others but in course of play it was evident that the bally machine was an one armed bandit, for it had gobbled up all his coins.

As Bir and Chet turned their attention towards the green baize of the roulette tables, a voice announced that the Keno game number four was just being started. Then the numbers started being also announced on the loudspeaker, and it was quite obvious that Bir was not going to make quick money by multiplying his Rs. 10 investment ten thousand times to make it one thousand rupees. Nevertheless he had four right, and as a consequence he got twenty rupees. With these earnings he went off to the roulette tables.

This was quite crowded mainly by Indians who had come to Kathmandu to spend their Dashahara or Dasain holidays. There was the tubby middle aged man, the sauve looking well dressed Sardarji and the giggling girl probably in her late teens, who was now having the first flutter of her life. Judging by the small coins in front of her she was certainly not having beginner's luck.

Bir decided that his investment would now be Rs. 1,000 to start with. His play with the free coupons had made him believe that though it was not exactly his day, he was nevertheless going to end up on the positive side of the line. No playing with rupee chips. It was with 101 chips of rupees ten value that he made his debut at the roulette table.

To tell the truth, Bir had never really taken roulette seriously. His feeling was that if one really wanted to play to win, then he must sit down with a good bag-full of money and play at times with virtually no limits. He was going to prove it by playing with these chips. Even if he spread it around within the thirty six figured rectangles, the chances of his getting thirty-six times the initial investment were quite good. Or, one put it on all 36, when the roulette wheel began to roll and the ball came to rest on the 0 or 00, even then one was still going to win but only his own bets. The wheel rolled, the bets were placed within the squares, on the sides on reds and on black, on evens and odds. A momnt of expectation—would he lose? No, his number had come up—he had won 36 times. Then he went for the lucky five and it won, then the lucky seven, and it won again for him. Bir on Chet's prompting went for seventeen but no luck. Hang it, thought Bir and went instead for the unlucky thirteen, putting no less then 10 of his discs. It won and made him feel great when the croupier pushed the stacks of chips to him. Was it a peculiar flair he had, which was the cause of his winning streak, he wondered? So the evening wore on. Bir won most of the time, lost on some occasions, but the sum total of it all was that he had cleaned up quite a bit from the Casino Nepal that night. His Rs. 1,000 had become Rs 10,000 in a few hours. Not had, Bir thought, for a start!

As they came out and walked back towards the foyer they saw that the genteel grey-haired lady had had quite a windfall, judging be the pile of coins by her side. The cold midnight air seemed to chill them to their bones as they came out of the Casino. Both Bir and Chet thought that the free whisky that they had had whilst they had been playiug had not been enough. They both got into the Casino provided car and started back towards the town, taking the short cut through the old part of the city. As luck would have it, they came across a procession going up the Bhimsenthan slope. There was no question of trying to by-pass or overtake it: the only recourse being to plod on in its wake. They could see in the illumination of the car's headlights the Gurju's troops, lanky, thin looking men carrying rifles; then behind this was a motley of men, and behind this yet another crowd who were holdlng up a huge image showing just the head and shoulders.

"What is this festival that is going on at this unearthly hour ?" Chet asked the driver of the car.

"It's Pachali Bhairab being taken to Hanuman Dhoka. Going in the precesion in front of him is the statue of Lord Ganesh."

"Well take us up to Hanuman Dhoka too. Let's see what happens. We will pay you for the extra journey," said Bir.

The Casino car driver knowing that one of these two

had won quite a bit at the tables was only too happy to oblige. The car followed the procession and the driver took them as near to Hanuman Dhoka as possible. Bir and Chet got out to have a look after telling the driver to wait for them at that spot.

The huge metallic head of Pachali Bhairab was taken near the image of Hanuman, the Monkey God, and set down. Then they heard a thud sound, and realised immediately that a male buffalo had had its head hacked off with a Gurkha scimitar. Bir saw the blood spurting out of the dead animal's headless body. Was this cruel ? Was this senseless ? He wondered. It was after all a part of the culture that he was born in and brought up on.

After all, what was life anyway ? There was the buffalo, alive a second ago but now lying there in front of the image of the Pachali Bhairab—a headless creature, its legs kicking in all directions. Would the buffalo, now that it had met its end for a noble cause, attain the right to be reborn as a human or not be born at all ? What about Bir himself ? Would he have to be re-born again, perhaps as lowly a creature as that Buffalo ? Bir was sure that he had not done enough good in this life to be able to attain Nirvana. For him the whole cycle of life still existed to be traversed yet another time.

Bir looked towards the buffalo and saw that the people there were now worshipping a man whom they called Ajinomo God. The man looked as if in a trance, probably as a result of the alcohol and of the repetitive droning noises made by the various musical instruments to produce that kind of atmosphere. Bir felt tired and worn out. Even if he was born again, even as that god forsaken buffalo, life would be better for him. He was fed up with this damn world, fed up to his gills. The procession had still to be taken back along the route it had come. Bir turned to Chet and said,

"Let's go back to your rooms at Thamel. We have had enough activity during these last few hours."

Bir's idea about not returning home for a few days was well fixed in his brain. True it was Dasain, and he, as the master of the house, should have given Tika to his wife and the children. He could not, however, bear the thought of going there when he was so flustered. He wondered whether he was doing the right thing—after all if one did not take Tika then it meant that the person concerned had no obligation to observe any mourning customs, He was himself giving Janaki adequate reason for not doing his last rites. If Janaki did not do it, then he had to make provision for alternative arrangements. With these thoughts through his mind, he gave the Rs. 10,000 earnings of the previous day to Chet and asked him to keep it, in case it would be required for his funeral and last rites.

"Don't give me all that money. After all, you know how money just slips through my hands. I might be tempted to spend it and since you are not going to die for some time yet, it might mean that I will have spent the whole thing by the time that it is actually required. You know my weaknesses Bir. Furthermore, what guarantee is there that I won't go before you, Bir ?"

"I know your weaknesses Chet. But I don't think that you will let me down. Even if you spent some of it I am sure that there would be enough left. And if they do, do my Arghan, you don't have to say a word about this money to anyone. It's yours for the keeping."

That next day however Janaki did come to Chet's lodging and did take her Tika from Bir. Bir felt that in her heart of hearts she really doted on him, but that it was the influence of Kipak which kept her back.

Janaki persuaded him to come with her back to their own house in Jamal. When they came there, Bir, however, sensed that all was still not well. and that the status quo was not regained. Kipak tried to give vent to his feelings by taking it out not only on him but also on poor Janaki. Bir kept quiet most of the time; and he tried to keep out of Kipak's way. After all, with Janaki pregnant, he did not want any more quarrels; for the strain of it might upset her to the extent of having a miscarriage and thus losing the baby. Bir felt now that his primary consideration was to protect her.

With this in mind Bir went to Chet and they went together to a lawyer. The idea was to put the money in trust with the lawyer and Chet as trustees under the existing Guthi laws. The terms were such that a certain amount of the interest only could be taken out every year, even Janaki not having control over the principle. Janaki would get an allowance for herself and her mentally defective son for the whole of their lives. It would be obligatory on her and perhaps on the new born son to perform Bir's arghan. This will was tight—water tight—and Bir felt that Kipak Tamang was now out of the picture.

It was as he had wished, anticipated and expected. A son was born but life became more intolerable for him. With the birth of this normal son, Janaki seemed to feel that she had more of a hold on him. Bir became more depressed; and Chet seeing this decided to take him to the hospital at Patan. The doctor was very kind and considerate, but the diagnosis was the same as before. Bir had tea with Chet at his rooms, and went from there towards the Swyambhunath stupa on the hillock at the western end of the Kathmandu valley.

The place had changed quite a bit since he had last been there. There were at the bottom of the hillock, two square shaped prayer houses, each containing huge prayer drums which were being revolved by the devotees as they went round it. Just a tap of the hand from each of that continuous stream of people was all that was required. Then Bir went past the colourfully painted stone images of the devotees, picking his way amongst the carved stone tablets or even the boulders, until he finally reached the top and stood in front of the huge stupa. As Bir said the words, 'Sange

Chom Khemde', he knew that he had made his peace with the world and had fallen at the feet of Lord Buddha. Scenes from his own life came surging into his mind. His life at Chetrafal Deurali, his days at Burma, his days in Nepal and his journeys to and fro. Had it been worthwhile? Bir doubted very much.

From Swyambhunath Stupa, Bir went back to the house at Jamal. In his coat pocket was the pistol that he taken from Chet's room. Except for the childern and the ten year old girl help, the house was empty—Kipak and Janaki having gone out to see a cinema. Bir went up to the room, bolted the door and pointing the pistol at his right temple, he pulled the trigger.

+ + + +

The ten year old girl heard a loud reverberating noise coming from the room upstairs. She ran to the door but it was bolted from the inside. As she came down the stairs wondering what to do, she realised that some neighbours, hearing the report of the pistol shot, had come to their house. They all went up the stairs, and tried to push open the door. One of the neighbours smelling fumes of the pistol went out to inform police.

It was the police, who when they arrived, had ultimately to break down the door. They found Bir dead on the floor, lying in a pool of his own blood. There was a note stating that he had stolen the pistol from his friend Chet and had decided to take his own life. There was also a note to Chet instructing him to request Janaki to do his arghan on the forty-ninth day of his death.

After Bir's body had been cremated at the Aryaghat of the Bagmati river, and after the thirteen days of kirya, were over, Chet brought up the question of the arghan. Janaki and Kipak both had a good laugh and said that any further spending by them was now out of the question. It was now their turn to collect after all these years of torture with Bir

Bahadur. Chet did not reply but went out of the house.

It was natural that when the contents of the will became known, it created a certain amount of stir. Janaki decided to contest it, and this, of course, was on the advise of Kipak. When the lawyer said and explained to her that it was not against her and her children that Bir had made such stipulation, she finally resigned herself to the terms and conditions.

Kipak was not ready to accept defeat so quickly. He reasoned and then quarrelled with Janaki. Finally when Kipak realised that there was no way whatsoever in which he could lay his hands on Janaki's money, he decided to leave her and seek a more willing victim. Janaki missed Kipak for a few days but then realised that it was all for the best. When Chet came to see her a few days after this episode, he found a different Janaki. It looked as if she had found peace at last. She told Chet that she had been a fool and had been so unkind to Bir who was her benefactor. But he was no more. She would try to make amends by bringing up the children in the way that he Bir would have liked her to. As Chet left the house he too felt that was exactly what Bir would have wished, had he been alive.

THE END

BURMESE TERMS

Amyunma———— Barren woman.

Balachow———— A fish preparation made with shrimps, onions and tomatoes, sometimes also fried.

Baluma———— Demons.

Bontai———— Shan lungi.

Cheroot———— Burmese cigar.

Chowme———— A precious stone, reddish in colour.

Gaungbaung———— Headgear of cloth worn on official occasions.

Mogok————Name of a place, also type of precious stone.

Ngapi———— A fish preparation used as delicacy in the form of a salted and pressed fish paste.

Phaya———— Gods.

Pongi———— Priests.

Punna———— Brahmin palmistry expert.

Rahan———— Monk.

Stapna————Founding or consecration of a pagoda.

Weza———— Wise men.